T0054981

Schopenhauer: A Very Short Introduction

VERY SHORT INTRODUCTIONS are for anyone wanting a stimulating and accessible way into a new subject. They are written by experts, and have been translated into more than 45 different languages.

The series began in 1995, and now covers a wide variety of topics in every discipline. The VSI library now contains over 500 volumes—a Very Short Introduction to everything from Psychology and Philosophy of Science to American History and Relativity—and continues to grow in every subject area.

Titles in the series include the following:

Christopher Janaway

SCHOPENHAUER

A Very Short Introduction

OXFORD
UNIVERSITY PRESS

OXFORD

UNIVERSITY PRESS

Great Clarendon Street, Oxford OX2 6DP

Oxford University Press is a department of the University of Oxford.
It furthers the University's objective of excellence in research, scholarship,
and education by publishing worldwide in

Oxford New York

Auckland Bangkok Buenos Aires Cape Town Chennai
Dar es Salaam Delhi Hong Kong Istanbul Karachi Kolkata
Kuala Lumpur Madrid Melbourne Mexico City Mumbai Nairobi
São Paulo Shanghai Taipei Tokyo Toronto

Oxford is a registered trade mark of Oxford University Press
in the UK and in certain other countries

Published in the United States
by Oxford University Press Inc., New York

British Library Cataloguing in Publication Data
Data available

Library of Congress Cataloging in Publication Data
Data available
ISBN 978-0-19-280259-0

Typeset by RefineCatch Ltd, Bungay, Suffolk
Printed and bound by
CPI Group (UK) Ltd, Croydon, CR0 4YY

Contents

Preface

This book aims to give a sympathetic but critical account of Schopenhauer's philosophy. He constructed a system which embraces metaphysics, epistemology, philosophy of mind, aesthetics, ethics, and the meaning of life. But as a complete system his philosophy has had few adherents, and he never founded a school of thought. His influence on the history of thought was rather that of provoking and inspiring generations of artists and thinkers from Wagner through to Wittgenstein. Some of his ideas prefigure those of Freud, and his most important philosophical impact was on Nietzsche, who at first found his pessimist conclusions attractive and later regarded them as repulsive, but was always in close dialogue with his 'great teacher'. Schopenhauer was a true atheist, who fundamentally questioned the value of human existence. Existence for Schopenhauer is a purposeless, painful striving, driven by an unconscious force that we cannot control. Release from this existence comes from losing one's individuality in aesthetic experience, in compassion for the world, and in self-denial. While examining all the main aspects of Schopenhauer's philosophical system, this book hopes to bring out the challenging nature of the questions he asks about human existence.

C. J.
August 2001

Abbreviations and works cited

Schopenhauer's works are referred to as follows, in translations by
E. F. J. Payne, unless otherwise stated. Some very minor changes are
made to some quoted passages.

B	*On the Basis of Morality* (1841; Bobbs-Merrill, 1965).
F	*On the Freedom of the Will* (1841), tr. K. Kolenda (Blackwell, 1985).
M1–M4	*Manuscript Remains*, vols. 1–4, ed. A. Hübscher (Berg Publishers, 1988–90).
N	*On the Will in Nature* (1836; Berg Publishers, 1992).
P1, P2	*Parerga and Paralipomena*, vols. 1 & 2 (1851, Clarendon Press, 1974).
R	*The Fourfold Root of the Principle of Sufficient Reason* (1813, 1847; Open Court, 1974).
W1, W2	*The World as Will and Representation*, vols. 1 & 2 (1819, 1844; Dover, 1969).

List of illustrations

1. Schopenhauer: daguerreotype, 4 June 1853

Chapter 1
Schopenhauer's life and works

Arthur Schopenhauer was born in 1788 in Danzig, and died in Frankfurt am Main in 1860. There are a number of photographs taken during the last decade of his life, from which we derive our most immediate sense of the man. He looks unconventional and grimly determined, but the sparkle in his eye is that of someone vigilant, incisive, and capable of mischief – not altogether different from the persona which emerges from his writings. At the end of his life Schopenhauer was just beginning to enjoy a measure of fame. His philosophy, however, is not a product of old or middle age. Although most of the words which he published were written after he settled in Frankfurt at the age of 45, it was in the years between 1810 and 1818 that he had produced the entire philosophical system for which he became celebrated. As Nietzsche later wrote, we should remember that it was the creative, rebellious energy of a man in his twenties which produced *The World as Will and Representation*. The mature Schopenhauer occupied himself in consolidating and supplementing the position he had presented in this masterpiece, which was, until very near the end of his life, neglected by the intellectual world.

Independence of spirit is the trait most characteristic of Schopenhauer. He writes fearlessly with little respect for authority, and detests the hollow conformism which he finds in the German academic establishment. But behind this is the significant fact that he was also financially independent. When he came of age in 1809, he inherited wealth which, with astute management, was sufficient to see him through the rest of his life. His father, Heinrich Floris Schopenhauer, had been one of the wealthiest businessmen in Danzig at the time of Arthur's birth. A cosmopolitan man, committed to the liberal values of the Enlightenment and to republicanism, he left Danzig when it was annexed by Prussia, and moved to the free city of Hamburg. Arthur had in common with his father a love of French and English culture and a horror of Prussian nationalism. The name 'Arthur' was chosen because it was shared by several European languages – though the intention here was chiefly to fit the infant for his envisaged career in pan-European commerce. Later Arthur felt he had also inherited his father's intense, obsessive personality. His father's death in 1805, probably by suicide, was a great blow to him.

Schopenhauer received a broad and enriching education in school, enhanced by the travel and social contacts that his wealthy family made possible. Sent to France at the age of 9 when his sister was born, he acquired fluent French. After some years of schooling, at the age of 15 he embarked with his parents on a two-year trip to Holland, England, France, Switzerland, and Austria. He saw many of the famous sights of the day, and at times was deeply affected by the poverty and suffering he witnessed. While his parents toured Britain, however, he was consigned to a boarding-school in Wimbledon, whose narrow, disciplinarian, religious outlook (a marked contrast to the education he had hitherto received) made a negative impression that was to last. This episode says much about Schopenhauer's character and upbringing. He was a seething, belligerent pupil who would not submit to the stultifying practices that surrounded him, and he seems quite isolated in his defiance. His parents wrote to him, his father niggling about his handwriting, his mother gushing about the wonderful time they were having and pleading with him to take a more reasonable attitude, but neither showed much inclination to see things from his point of view. It is tempting to view the situation as a microcosm of his later life. As his life progressed, it became clearer that it would not be constructed around close relationships with others. He began to see company as like a fire 'at which the prudent man warms himself at a distance' (M1, 123), and resolved to be lonely even when with others, for fear of losing his own integrity. He later wrote that five-sixths of human beings were worth only contempt, but equally saw that there were inner obstacles to human contact: 'Nature has done more than is necessary to isolate my heart, in that she endowed it with suspicion, sensitiveness, vehemence and pride' (M4, 506). He was prone to depression, and confessed 'I always have an anxious concern that causes me to see and look for dangers where none exist' (M4, 507).

Some writers on Schopenhauer's personality have looked to his relationships with his parents, and what they have found is not surprising. His father was an anxious, exacting, and formidable man, very ambitious for his son. Johanna Schopenhauer, née Trosiener, also from a successful business family in Danzig, was quite different. A lively, sociable person, she had literary aspirations, which culminated in a career as a romantic novelist, making her during her lifetime more famous than her son. She was a significant force in his life, but relations between them were never warm. In her marriage too, as she herself wrote, she saw no need to 'feign ardent love' for her husband, adding that he did not expect it. After Heinrich Schopenhauer died, the independently minded Johanna was free to embark on her own career, and moved to Weimar, where she established an artistic and intellectual salon frequented by many of the luminaries of the day. Arthur benefited from some of the relationships he established in this circle, notably with Goethe, and with the oriental scholar Friedrich Majer, who stimulated in him a life-long interest in Indian thought. However, his relationship with his mother became stormy, and in 1814 she threw him out for good, never to see him again.

By the time this happened Schopenhauer had abandoned the career in business which his father had projected for him, and had found his way into the life of learning. In 1809 he went to the University at Göttingen, from where he was to move on to Berlin two years later. He attended lectures on a variety of scientific subjects, having originally intended to study medicine; but he soon gravitated towards philosophy. The Göttingen philosopher G. E. Schulze played a decisive role in Schopenhauer's career when he advised him to begin by reading the works of Plato and Kant. Though Schopenhauer was, by any standards, a widely read and scholarly thinker, it is fair to say that his reading of these two philosophers provoked in him the fundamental ideas that shaped his philosophy from then on. The Hindu Upanishads, which he learned of through Friedrich Majer, were the third ingredient which he later blended with Platonic and Kantian elements to make something quite original in *The World as Will and Representation*.

When he moved to Berlin, Schopenhauer heard lectures by Schleiermacher and Fichte, two of the philosophical heavyweights of the day, though, true to form, he was fairly contemptuous of them, and certainly did not seem to think he was there to absorb what they had to say. His lecture notes and marginal annotations to the books he was reading (preserved in *Manuscript Remains*) show him keen to object and debate, and, for a young student, he reacts with an almost uncanny sureness of his own position. This too is a pattern that was not to vary greatly. Schopenhauer did not learn in association with others, by exchanging ideas and submitting himself to scrutiny. He learned, and wrote, by relying on his own judgement and treating other people's ideas as raw material to be hammered into the shape he wanted. What he could not use he sometimes decried as rubbish, with a witty style of mockery that usually succeeds in keeping the reader on his side. Schopenhauer would have made far less of himself without such single-minded determination, but the same feature has its compensating weakness: it can be a virtue for a philosopher to exhibit more give and take, more sense of dialogue and self-criticism, than Schopenhauer sometimes does.

When Schopenhauer was ready to write his doctoral thesis, in 1813, war broke out. Schopenhauer had an aversion to fighting, and even more of an aversion to fighting on the Prussian side against the French. He fled south to Rudolstadt near Weimar and there completed his first work, *On the Fourfold Root of the Principle of Sufficient Reason*, which gained him his doctorate at Jena, and was published in an edition of 500 copies in the same year. The book takes a stock academic topic, the principle of sufficient reason (which says that, for everything that is, there must be a ground or reason why it is), lays out concisely the ways in which it has been dealt with in the history of philosophy, then proceeds to a four-part explanation of the different kinds of reason. The systematic framework is derived from Kant, whose thought Schopenhauer has clearly assimilated, though not uncritically. There are enough twists to make this the beginning of something new, and more than a hint of what is to come in his major work. Schopenhauer always considered *The Fourfold Root* essential to understanding his thought, and undertook a revision of it for re-publication in 1847.

Another early publication is the essay *On Vision and Colours*, of 1816. This short book is a product of his involvement with Goethe, whose anti-Newtonian theory of colours had been published at the beginning of the decade. In discussing this theory, Schopenhauer and Goethe came to know each other quite well. Schopenhauer did not regard it as a central project of his own, but understandably did not turn down the invitation to work with one of the greatest men he was ever likely to meet. Goethe, forty years his senior, recognized the rigour of Schopenhauer's mind, and regarded him as someone with great potential, but was less concerned to foster his talent than to receive help in his own intellectual endeavours. The brief period in which they worked together is the one exceptional collaboration in Schopenhauer's career – but still he did not have it in him to become anyone's disciple. His own work *On Vision and Colours* diverged somewhat from Goethe's thinking, and he did not disguise the fact that he thought it superior. The partnership tailed off, Schopenhauer disappointed, though not crushed, by Goethe's lukewarm response. He later sent Goethe a copy of *The World as Will and Representation*, and had an apparently cordial meeting with him in 1819. But by now the two had parted company. As Goethe was to say, they were like two people who eventually shook hands, one turning to go south, the other north.

Schopenhauer's true destination is revealed in Volume I of *The World as Will and Representation*, which he completed in Dresden and published in 1818, although 1819 is the date that stands on the title-page. The dispassionate, Kantian exercise which Schopenhauer carried out in *The Fourfold Root* of 1813 did not reveal the driving force of his philosophy. It did not address questions concerning suffering and salvation, ethics and art, sexuality, death, and the meaning of life, but it was in these areas that his preoccupations already lay. The collected *Manuscript Remains* show Schopenhauer's greatest book in a process of composition over a period of almost ten years. Adapting the thought of both Plato and Kant, he had become convinced that there was a split between ordinary consciousness and a higher or 'better' state in which the human mind could pierce beyond mere appearances to a knowledge of something more real. The thought had aesthetic and religious overtones: Schopenhauer wrote of both the artist and the 'saint' as possessing this 'better consciousness' – though it should be said straightaway that his philosophical system is atheist through and through. He also struck one of the keynotes of pessimism, saying that the life of ordinary experience, in which we strive and desire and suffer, is something from which to be liberated. Such thoughts were well established in Schopenhauer's mind by 1813.

The idea which allowed his monumental book to take shape was his conception of the will. In the finished work, as its title indicates, Schopenhauer presents the world as having two sides, that of *Vorstellung* (representation), or the way things present themselves to us in experience, and that of *Wille* (will), which is, he argues, what the world is in *itself*, beyond the mere appearances to which human

2. Schopenhauer as a youth, 1802

knowledge is limited. The will is not easy to define. It is, to begin with, easier to say what it is not. It is not any kind of mind or consciousness, nor does it direct things to any rational purpose (otherwise 'will' would be another name for God). Schopenhauer's world is purposeless. His notion of will is probably best captured by the notion of *striving towards* something, provided one remembers that the will is fundamentally 'blind', and found in forces of nature which are without consciousness at all. Most importantly, the human psyche can be seen as split: comprising not only capacities for understanding and rational thought, but at a deeper level also an essentially 'blind' process of striving, which governs, but can also conflict with, the conscious portions of our nature. Humanity is poised between the life of an organism driven to survival and reproduction, and that of a pure intellect that can rebel against its nature and aspire to a timeless contemplation of a 'higher' reality.

Though he does still envisage a kind of resigned 'salvation', Schopenhauer thinks ordinary existence must involve the dual miseries of pain and boredom, insisting that it is in the very essence of humanity, indeed of the world as a whole, that it should be so.

Many have found Schopenhauer's philosophy impossible to accept as a single, consistent metaphysical scheme. But it does have great strength and coherence as a narrative and in the dynamic interplay between its different conceptions of the world and the self. What is set down at the beginning should be treated not so much as a foundation for everything that is to come, but as a first idea which will be revealed as inadequate by a second that seems to undermine it, only to reassert itself in transformed guise later on. There is a superficial resemblance here to the method of his contemporary Hegel, though everything to do with Hegel was anathema to Schopenhauer, and in other respects they could hardly differ more as writers. Thomas Mann likened Schopenhauer's book to a great symphony in four movements, and it is helpful to approach it in something of this spirit, seeking contrasts of mood and unities of theme amid a wealth of variations. Certainly there have been few philosophers who have equalled Schopenhauer's grasp of literary architecture and pacing, and few whose prose style is so eloquent.

For all this, the great work went virtually unnoticed for many years after its publication. Schopenhauer was embittered, but he was not one to think that the world was right and he was wrong; he continued throughout his life to believe in the supreme value of his work. In 1820 he was awarded the right to lecture at the University in Berlin, after speaking before a gathering of the faculty chaired by Hegel, the professor of philosophy. Schopenhauer duly presented himself to lecture, under the stunning title 'The whole of philosophy, i.e. the theory of the essence of the world and of the human mind'. But he had chosen to speak at the same time as Hegel. Two hundred attended the lecture of the professor, who was at the peak of his career, and the unknown Schopenhauer was left with a pitiful few. His name was on the lecture-schedule in later years, but he never returned to repeat the experience, and this was the end of his lecturing career. Hegel was the epitome of everything that Schopenhauer disliked in philosophy. He was a career academic, who made use of the institutional authority which Schopenhauer held in contempt. He upheld the church and the state, for which Schopenhauer, an atheist and an individualist, had no time. Although thoroughly conservative himself, Schopenhauer regarded the political state merely as a convenient means for protecting property and curbing the excesses of egoism; he could not stomach Hegel's representation of the state as 'the whole aim of human existence' (*P1*, 147). Hegel was also an appalling stylist, who seemed to build abstraction upon abstraction without the breath of fresh air provided by common-sense experience, and Schopenhauer – not alone in this – found his writing pompous and obscurantist, even dishonest. The emblem at the head of Hegelian university philosophy, he says, should be 'a cuttle-fish creating a cloud of obscurity around itself so that no one sees what it is, with the legend, *mea caligine tutus* (fortified by my own obscurity)' (*N*, 24). It is not true to say that Schopenhauer's philosophy was based on opposition to Hegel – Hegel was far from his mind as he created his major work – but Hegel's triumphant success, coupled with his own continuing lack of recognition, nevertheless produced in him a rancour which dominated much of his subsequent career.

During the 1820s Schopenhauer was at his least productive. He travelled to Italy, suffered during and after his return journey from serious illness and depression, and continued an affair with Caroline Richter, a chorus girl at the National Theatre in Berlin. He planned a number of writing projects, such as translations of Hume's works on religion and of Sterne's *Tristram Shandy*, but nothing came of them. His notebooks were filled, sometimes with invective against Hegelianism which he reworked for inclusion in later works, but he completed no more publications while in Berlin. It is especially sad that the English publisher he approached about translating Kant's *Critique of Pure Reason* and other works should have turned him down. Schopenhauer's English was good, his feel for literary form superb, and his knowledge of Kant's work intimate. One can only speculate how the history of ideas would have been affected had he succeeded in making Kant more accessible to the English-speaking world at this comparatively early date. (By contrast, a result of his scholarship to which we are indebted is the rediscovery of the first edition of the *Critique*, which was republished in 1838 partly thanks to his efforts.)

In 1831 cholera reached Berlin, apparently claiming Hegel among its victims, and Schopenhauer left the city. After some indecision he settled in Frankfurt, where he was to continue living an outwardly uneventful life, balanced between writing and recreation – theatre, opera, walking, playing the flute, dining out, and reading *The Times* in the town's library. Now he was able to produce more books. In 1836 he published *On the Will in Nature*, which was designed to support his doctrine of the will by putting forward corroborative scientific evidence from independent sources. It is still a work of interest, although arguably it does not stand very well on its own apart from *The World as Will and Representation*. However, in 1838 and 1839 Schopenhauer entered for two essay competitions set by the Norwegian Royal Scientific Society and its Danish counterpart, and the two occasions produced a pair of fine self-standing essays, *On the Freedom of the Will* and *On the Basis of Morality*, which were published together in 1841 under the title *The Two Fundamental Problems of Ethics*. In terms of doctrine these pieces are not radical departures from his earlier work, but both are well-constructed and persuasive pieces in which local parts of the grand design are presented with clarity. They can readily be recommended to a student of ethics today. In the essay on freedom Schopenhauer presents a convincing case for determinism, only to say, as some more recent philosophers have, that the deeper issues of freedom and responsibility are scarcely resolved thereby. This essay was rewarded with a gold medal by the Norwegians.

3. Schopenhauer: miniature portrait by Karl Ludwig Kaaz, 1809

The second essay, part of which is a thorough criticism of Kant's ethics, suffered a different fate in Denmark: despite its being the only entry, the Royal Society refused to award it a prize. It had not, they judged, successfully answered the question set – and they took exception to the 'unseemly' manner in which a number of recent philosophers of distinction had been referred to. Who did they mean? asked Schopenhauer in his Preface to the essays: Fichte and Hegel! Are these men the *summi philosophi* one is not allowed to insult? It is true that Schopenhauer had not been playing the conventional game of academic politeness, but now he seizes the chance to let rip with all the means at his command. He produces an escalating series of allegations about the emptiness and confusion of Hegel's philosophy, throwing in a picturesque quote from Homer about the chimera, which is a compound of many beasts, and ending

> Further, if I were to say that this *summus philosophus* of the Danish Academy scribbled nonsense quite unlike any mortal before him, so that whoever could read his most eulogized work, the so-called *Phenomenology of Mind*, without feeling as if he were in a madhouse, would qualify as an inmate for Bedlam, I should be no less right. (*B*, 16)

In 1844 a second volume of *The World as Will and Representation* was published along with a new edition of the first volume. Schopenhauer was wise in not trying to rewrite his youthful work. What he provides instead is a substantial elaboration of the original, clarifying and extending it with the benefit of mature reflection. The second volume is actually longer than the first, and the two combine well to produce a single work. They were published together again in a third edition in 1859, the year before he died. Schopenhauer's final new publication was another two-volume book, entitled *Parerga and Paralipomena*, which appeared in 1851. The imposing title means 'complementary works and matters omitted', and the contents range from extended philosophical essays to the more popular 'Aphorisms on the Wisdom of Life', which have often been published separately. Somewhat strangely, it was this late work, which was reviewed favourably first in England, that led to Schopenhauer's becoming well known. There was demand for new editions of his writings, and he even became a topic for German university courses. He received many visitors, and much correspondence, including the complete libretto of *The Ring of the Nibelung* from an ardent fan, Richard Wagner, of whose music, incidentally, he did not think very highly. In the first fifty years after his death Schopenhauer was to become one of the most influential writers of Europe. Though he made no claim to be a poet, the verses which came to stand at the very end of *Parerga and Paralipomena* (P2, 658) are no doubt an honest reflection of what he felt in his last years:

1856

Finale

I now stand weary at the end of the road;
The jaded brow can hardly bear the laurel.
And yet I gladly see what I have done,
Ever undaunted by what others say.

4. Schopenhauer: photograph by Johann Schäfer, April 1859

Chapter 2
Within and beyond appearance

Appearance and thing in itself

Schopenhauer's philosophical thinking is easiest to grasp if one first sees the backbone that runs right through it. This is the distinction, which he found in Kant, between appearance and thing in itself. The world of appearance consists of things as we know them by the ordinary means of sense experience and scientific investigation, in other words the empirical world. Appearance is not to be understood as straightforward illusion: the things that meet us in our empirical knowledge are not hallucinations, but to use the Greek word for appearances, they are the phenomena that make up the world. However, there is still the question whether the whole world consists only of these phenomena. Should we regard 'what there is' as being exhausted by our empirical knowledge? We can at least conceive of a reality independent of what we could experience, and this is what Kant meant by talking of things 'in themselves'.

Kant's achievement was to show that knowledge was limited: we could never know how the world was in itself, only how it could appear to us, as scientists or ordinary perceivers. The pretensions of traditional metaphysicians to know about God, the immortality of the soul, or a supernatural order pervading the whole universe were therefore doomed. According to Schopenhauer's assessment (in his 'Critique of the Kantian Philosophy' [Appendix to *W1*, 417–25]), Kant had added to this destructive achievement two others that were more positive. The first was the idea that the world of appearance had fundamental and necessary organizing principles which could be discovered. The second was the view that ethics could be separated off from the sphere of appearance, and was not knowledge in the way that science was: when considering ourselves as beings who must act and judge things to be right or wrong, we were not dealing with how matters lay in the empirical world.

First, let us take the idea that appearance, the world as we know it, has a necessary structure. Kant thought that the world of appearance must occupy space and time. It is obviously hard to imagine there not being space or time, but Kant went further and argued that without them there could not be a knowable world at all. A similar point applies to cause and effect, and to the principle that things can endure unchanged through time. The rules of the empirical world are that it must contain enduring things, arranged in space and time, and having systematic effects upon one another. Nothing else, Kant argued, could ever count as an empirical world that we could know. However, his most startling claim is that all these rules are not present in the world as it is in itself. They are all rules simply about how the world must be *if* we are to be able to experience it. So space and time, cause and effect, relate only to the way in which things have to appear to us. Take away the experiencing subject, and none of the world's structure would remain.

The second positive point from Kant concerns our view of ourselves. As well as trying to understand the world, we are called upon to act and make decisions, and these will ultimately be governed by questions of morality. Kant argues that morality can work only if each of us conceives himself or herself purely as a rational being, who is constrained by duty, and has freedom to choose the principles on which he or she will act. No kind of empirical investigation could reveal us to be such purely rational, free beings: if you like, there are no such things in the physical world.

15

Nevertheless, it is a conception of ourselves which we must have. So, even though my knowledge is limited to the empirical world, I cannot ever believe that what I am is limited in the same way. Kant's idea, simply put, is that I must think that *in myself*, beyond appearances, I am a free and purely rational agent.

Now when Schopenhauer came across the Kantian philosophy as a student at Göttingen, he found it convincing, but incomplete. He embraced the distinction between appearance and thing in itself. On the appearance side, he wanted to modify Kant's views, but was happy to agree that the empirical world did not exist in itself, and was given its structure by rules of space, time, and causality imposed by us. It was, however, on the side of the thing in itself that he felt Kant had fudged his account. What is the world really, in itself? And what am I? This was the double riddle which Kant had left by distinguishing appearance from thing in itself, and claiming that it was only of appearances that one could have knowledge. The conception of the thing in itself gave rise to other philosophical problems which had been much discussed in the German academic world. Both Schopenhauer's first teacher, Schulze, and Fichte, whose lectures he heard in Berlin, were prominent in the debate. In presenting his solution to the riddle, claiming that the thing in itself, both in the world and in the microcosm of the human being, was *will*, Schopenhauer was addressing a burning problem of the day, and to some extent trading on a familiar post-Kantian idea.

The better consciousness

At the beginning, the young Schopenhauer was reading not only Kant, but also Plato, and here he encountered another way of understanding the difference between what appears and what 'really is'. What 'really is' for Plato is a set of unchanging entities called Ideas or Forms. Individual things are imperfect, they come and go, but this does not affect the fundamental order in the universe, which is constituted by absolute and eternal Forms. Plato thought that the greatest achievement for humanity would be to gain an understanding of these eternal Forms, such as Justice itself, Goodness itself, and Beauty itself. The human soul would be elevated to a plane where it transcended the limitations of mere opinion and mortal appetite, gained an apprehension of absolute standards of value, and achieved a release from conflict and suffering. At a crucial phase in his development Schopenhauer succumbed to this vision. Even though the Kantian thing in itself was supposed to be beyond the limits of human knowledge, while Plato's Ideas were the objects of knowledge *par excellence*, Schopenhauer conflated what the two were saying, and formed a Platonic view about what an insight into the thing in itself beyond appearance would be like. For many years he thought he had made an important discovery: '*Plato's Ideas* and *Kant's thing-in-itself* . . . that these two are one and the same is as unheard of as it is sure and certain' (*M1*, 377). Although he did come to see that the positions of the two great philosophers were in fact distinct, the fusion created in his mind had acquired an energy of its own. He believed that empirical consciousness, limited as it was to the phenomena of space, time, and causality, was something inferior which we should aspire to escape from, if possible. Only if there was a 'better' consciousness could human beings find anything that was of true value.

The term 'better consciousness' appears only in Schopenhauer's earliest unpublished manuscripts. It was not a very well-focused concept, and he abandoned it. But his later ideas about the value of art and about resigned detachment from life are continuous with his early view. In 1813, for example, he wrote the following in his notebooks:

> As soon as we *objectively consider, i.e. contemplate* the things of the world, then for the moment *subjectivity* and thus the source of all misery has vanished. We are free and the consciousness of the material world of the senses stands before us as something strange and foreign which no longer wears us down. Also we are no longer involved in considering the nexus of space, time and causality (useful for our individuality), but see

the Platonic Idea of the object ... This liberation from temporal consciousness leaves the better eternal consciousness behind. (M1, 50)

Ordinary consciousness is seen as something to which 'misery' attaches; if only we can break the Kantian rules that limit knowledge to appearance, we shall enter into a realm in which both we ourselves and the objects of our direct 'contemplation' are timeless. This 'liberation' Schopenhauer thinks may be found in art, and in the attitude to the world which he calls that of the 'saint'. Both the artistic genius and the saint supposedly contemplate reality from a standpoint which transcends ordinary empirical understanding. Many recent commentators have played down the influence of Plato, and treated Schopenhauer as a rather unorthodox Kantian. But the 'better consciousness' is dramatically un-Kantian; Schopenhauer's own assessment that Kant and Plato were united in his philosophy is nearer the mark, even if the two make themselves felt in quite different ways.

In fact, Schopenhauer was prone to cite three influences: 'I do not believe my doctrine could have come about before the Upanishads, Plato and Kant could cast their rays simultaneously into the mind of one man' (M1, 467). What of the third influence? Schopenhauer's knowledge of Plato and Kant, and his notion of the 'better consciousness', were already formed when he encountered the Upanishads, the sacred Hindu writings which he acquired in 1814 (in a Latin version taken from the Persian and entitled *Oupnek'hat)* and which he described in his late years as 'the consolation of my life' (P2, 397). We may note two principal ideas which impressed Schopenhauer in the Hindu writings he studied: one is Mâyâ or illusion, the other the identity of the individual with the world as a whole, embodied in the powerful Sanskrit saying '*tat tvam asi*' ('this art thou'). Schopenhauer often refers to our ordinary experience as not penetrating the 'veil of *Mâyâ*'. This is not the common sceptical thought that we cannot trust our senses to tell us about the material world, but rather the idea that the material world of our experience is not something eternal, and not something we should ultimately put our trust in. Schopenhauer thinks that the world of material things which we experience and can investigate in science must be cast aside as of no genuine worth by comparison with the timeless vision open to artists and saints. The suspension, or denial, of one's complete differentiation from the rest of the world ('this art thou') will be a feature of that timeless vision. Schopenhauer had to work out how one's understanding of both the world and the self would be transformed on abandoning ordinary empirical consciousness, and what came to play a central role here was the notion of losing the sense of oneself as a separate individual. Some of his ideas have a kinship with Buddhism which he later emphasized, though the relationship here was one of convergence rather than influence (*W2*, 169).

The Fourfold Root

While all these thoughts began to form, Schopenhauer set himself to write his doctoral dissertation, *On the Fourfold Root of the Principle of Sufficient Reason*. In it he makes no mention of the 'better consciousness', and deals simply with the principles governing ordinary experience and reasoning. He was obviously satisfied with the answers he reached, since he later retained them substantially unchanged, and frequently refers back to the dissertation. The fact that he produced an expanded version of the dissertation in 1847 confirms his statement that it is to be considered part of his complete system of thought. The text of *The Fourfold Root* we usually read today is this later version.

Schopenhauer begins *The Fourfold Root* with the single principle of sufficient reason which was the stock-in-trade of the eighteenth-century academic tradition associated with Leibniz and Christian Wolff. The principle states simply: 'Nothing is without a ground or reason why it is' (*R*, 6). Nothing is self-standing; everything is in relation to something else which is the reason for its being, or the explanation of it. However, there are, according to Schopenhauer, four distinct ways in which something may relate to a ground or reason, associated with four different kinds of explanation, which, he claims, none of his predecessors has clearly distinguished. The most familiar kind are causal or physical explanations, where we explain one event or state in terms of its relation to another which caused it. Then there are cases where we explain why some judgement is true by relating it to the grounds for its truth, such as an empirical observation or another truth from which it can be inferred. Thirdly, there are mathematical explanations – in which we explain, for example, why a triangle has the properties it does. Finally, there is explanation of what people do. We explain actions by relation to motives, which are their reasons, or causes, or both. In all these cases we are dealing with relations imposed by the mind, Schopenhauer thinks, and in each case the relation is one of necessity. Hence, in his terms, there are physical necessity, logical necessity, mathematical necessity, and moral necessity. Once we understand what the mind is doing when it operates with these relationships, we will have understood the forms that all explanation takes, and hence the true significance of the principle of sufficient reason. Let us deal with the four kinds of relation in turn.

By far the most substantial section of *The Fourfold Root* is devoted to the principle of causal explanation. An obvious class of objects the mind can grasp is that of the particular perceptible things that occupy space and time, and make up empirical reality. Space and time, as we saw, provide the basic structure of empirical reality. But space and time are not perceivable; what we can perceive is what fills space and time, and that, for Schopenhauer, is simply matter (*R*, 46). Were there not both time and space, there could be neither distinct material things nor change, and so nothing for causality to apply to. Now the principle of causality states that every change in the world of material things must have a cause, or, as Schopenhauer puts it, 'every state that appears must have ensued or resulted from a change that preceded it' (*R*, 53). The principle allows of no exceptions: what we usually call the cause of some event is merely a particular change that preceded it, but that change must itself have ensued from some previous changes, and so on. By ensuing,

Schopenhauer means following regularly, or 'as often as the first state exists'. Cause and effect are related in such a way that, if the first occurs, the second cannot but occur. This relation is seen as one of necessity.

Schopenhauer has a simple, uncluttered view about the nature of empirical reality. Individual material things exist in space and time. A material thing is something capable of interacting causally with other material things. And every change that occurs to a material thing is the necessary result of some preceding change that occurs to a material thing. One complication, however, is that Schopenhauer is not a realist about material things, but an idealist: that is, material things would not exist, for him, without the mind. He holds, with Kant, that the whole structure we have just described exists only as something presented to us as subjects, not in itself. When Schopenhauer says that empirical things in space and time are objects, he means that they are *objects for* a *subject*. 'Object' in his parlance means something met with in experience, or in the subject's consciousness. Space and time are the fundamental forms brought to experience by us. So the material occupants of space and time would not exist if it were not for the subject, and the causal connections which obtain between the states of material things are connections which we, as subjects, impose.

In Schopenhauer's account of perception, the human intellect 'creates' the world of ordinary material things (R, 75), and does so by applying the principle of cause and effect to sensations received by our bodily senses. We apprehend some change in our bodily state. The intellect then applies the principle of causality, and projects as cause of the sensation a material object 'outside' in space – and this projection is the object which we say we perceive. Thus the principle of causality is doubly important to Schopenhauer: it not only governs all interaction between material things, but is responsible for our construction of those very material things in the first place. The account has a certain ingenuity, but is troubling. For one thing, where do bodily sensations

21

come from? They must surely be originally caused in the body by something prior to the operation of the intellect, but Schopenhauer does not discuss what that prior cause might be. Secondly, how do we apprehend the initial sensation? It cannot be that the mind perceives the sensation as a change in a material thing (the body), and yet if it does not do so, why is the principle of causality, which governs changes of material things, called into operation at all?

Schopenhauer's second class of objects for the mind is made up of *concepts*. Concepts are, for Schopenhauer, mental representations which are by nature secondary: he calls them 'representations of representations'. The basic representations are experiences of things in the material world, such as a particular tree; the concept *tree* is, by contrast, a general representation formed to stand for many such objects, by leaving out the detailed elements of what is experienced in each case. Schopenhauer is fond of emphasizing that concepts are always at least one step removed from direct experience, for which he uses the Kantian term *Anschauung* (intuition or perception). He thinks that a concept, to be of much use to us, must always be capable of being cashed out in terms of experience. Concepts such as *being, essence*, or *thing*, have the least cash value in these terms (*R*, 147, 155). As we shall see, Schopenhauer also takes the view that in some areas, such as art and ethics, abstract conceptual thinking can actually stand in the way of genuine insight.

Nevertheless, possession of concepts is a distinctively human characteristic for Schopenhauer, raising us above the consciousness of which other animals are capable. Other creatures, in his view, can have a perception of material things existing in space and time, much as we do – in a remarkable passage he laments the fact that 'in the West where [man's] skin has turned white' we have ceased to acknowledge our kinship with animals whom we demean as 'beasts or brutes' (*R*, 146). But the other animals do lack conceptual representations, and so lack the ability to make judgements, to reason, to have a language, or

5. Schopenhauer: portrait by Ludwig Sigismund Ruhl, around 1818

an understanding of past and future. Thinking, or making judgements, is the fundamental function of concepts. Schopenhauer calls a judgement a combination or relationship of concepts, though he is not very clear about what this relationship involves. He is more interested in the idea that a judgement can express knowledge, and it is here that the principle of sufficient reason comes in again. 'If a judgement is to express a piece of *knowledge*, it must have a sufficient ground or reason; by virtue of this quality, it then receives the predicate *true*. *Truth* is therefore the reference of a judgement to something different therefrom' (*R*, 156). It is a familiar thought that a judgement amounts to knowledge if it is true and sufficiently grounded in something outside itself. Schopenhauer's brief remarks appear to make no distinction between a judgement's having a sufficient ground and its being true. Whether he would accept a notion of truth as correspondence with the way things are, independently of grounds for judging them to be so, remains obscure.

What Schopenhauer succeeds in establishing is that true judgements may be grounded in quite different ways. They may be grounded in another judgement, as when we argue, conclude, or infer (*R*, 157–8) from one truth to another. They may, on the other hand, be 'empirical truths', grounded not in another judgement, but in experience. For example, our judgement 'There is snow on the trees' may have its justification in the evidence of our senses. On the other hand in the syllogism 'There is snow on the trees. Snow is a white substance. Therefore, there is a white substance on the trees.' the truth of the final judgement is grounded simply in the truths of the two premisses. Schopenhauer calls this a 'logical' or 'formal' truth, meaning simply one whose ground is based on deduction, rather than observation. There are two other kinds of truth in his account, which he calls transcendental truth and metalogical truth. These occur respectively when a judgement is founded on the conditions of experience or on the conditions of thought in general. A notable transcendental truth is 'Nothing happens without a cause', which is neither grounded in observation nor on deduction from any other truths, but is an underlying principle on which all experience is based. (Schopenhauer is here following Kant closely.) Metalogical truths are supposedly a kind of judgement where, if we try to go against them, we cease to be able to think properly at all. One example Schopenhauer gives is 'No predicate can be simultaneously attributed and denied to a subject': we cannot think, for example, 'Snow is and is not white.' The principle of sufficient reason itself is a truth of this kind, Schopenhauer claims, though in some of its guises, especially the principle of causality, it appears as a transcendental truth (*R*, 162).

Schopenhauer's third class of objects in *The Fourfold Root* is made up simply of space and time. Once again, we are close to Kant, who thought that we can have knowledge not only of the particular things that fill space and time, but of the basic properties of space and time as such. Geometry and arithmetic, on this view, are bodies of knowledge concerning position in space and succession in time, but they are neither scientific empirical knowledge, nor a matter of mere logical deduction. With this view of geometry and arithmetic, which would now be disputed, Kant arrived at the idea that we must be able to grasp space and time in a pure, non-empirical way in our minds. Schopenhauer follows suit, and produces his third form of the principle of sufficient reason. The relation between a triangle's having three sides and its having three angles, for example, is that the one is grounded in, is a sufficient reason for, the other. But, Schopenhauer argues, this relation is not that between cause and effect, and is not that between a piece of knowledge and its justification either. We must distinguish not only the ground of becoming (change grounded in causes) and the ground of knowing (knowledge-claims grounded in justifications), but also the ground of being. If we say that a triangle has three angles because it has three sides, the ground we are referring to is simply the way that space, or one facet of it, is.

The final form of the principle of sufficient reason has application to only a single object for each subject. Each of us can be aware of himself or herself as a subject of will. We experience our own states of wanting and making decisions, and can always ask 'why?' (R, 212). Our willing, we assume, is preceded by something which is its ground, and which explains our action or decision. This prior something is what Schopenhauer calls a *motive*, and the principle in operation is what he terms the 'law of motivation', or the principle of the sufficient reason of acting. It states simply that every act of will can be explained as ensuing from some motive. The connection between motive and act of will is one of cause and effect, the same as holds universally for changes in the material world. Motivation is thus, as Schopenhauer puts it, 'causality seen from within' (R, 214).

The limits of sufficient reason

The Fourfold Root is a remarkable sustained attempt to separate different forms of explanation which the tradition before Schopenhauer had not always distinguished. We may certainly sympathize with his request that henceforth 'every philosopher, who in his speculations bases a conclusion on the principle of sufficient reason or ground, or indeed speaks of a ground at all, should be required to state what kind of ground he means' (R, 233). However, clarifying the framework which governs our experience and reasoning was only one part of Schopenhauer's task. He remarks in the enlarged edition of 1847 that none of the relationships he has dealt with applies beyond the phenomena out of which our experience is composed: the principle of sufficient reason would not apply in any of its forms to the world considered as thing in itself (R, 232–3). He also reminds us that 'the sublime Plato' degrades phenomenal reality to what is 'always only arising and passing away, but never really and truly existing' (R, 232).

In his 1813 notebooks Schopenhauer returned to his task of revealing what lay beyond all these subject-imposed modes of connection. Now something of great importance occurred: as he proceeded in his investigations, it became clear that revealing the nature of the thing in itself and clarifying the 'better' Platonic consciousness were two distinct enterprises. The thing in itself was a hidden essence working away underneath the order we imposed on the objects of our experience. It was also his own inner nature, something in him that drove him on – it was the world, as it were, surging up within him. To this hidden nature he gave the name will, and with it he now associated the 'misery' which ordinary life had to offer. By contrast, if only he could cease *being* this will, and cease imposing all subjective forms of connection, the same world would take on a wholly different aspect, revealing itself spread out before him in timeless objective glory as a panoply of Platonic Ideas. Schopenhauer's philosophy really took shape once he attained this distinction between thing in itself (will) and Platonic Ideas: the first the murky reality underlying the empirical world in which the individual toils and tries to understand the connections of things, the other an exceptional vision to aspire to, of all connections undone and a brighter reality contemplated without striving and pain.

Chapter 3
The world as will and representation

Schopenhauer's greatest work, *The World as Will and Representation*, is divided into four books, with a long appendix on Kant's philosophy in Volume I. Each of the four books sets out a distinct movement of thought. The first presents the world as representation, or as it is for our experience. The second book adds that this same world (and we ourselves within it) must be viewed under another aspect, as will. We called the appearance/thing in itself distinction the backbone of Schopenhauer's philosophy: now 'the world as representation' is what falls on the 'appearance' side of this line, while 'the world as will' is the thing in itself. But then in Book 3 aesthetic contemplation emerges as a cessation of willing in the individual, which transforms the world of objects into a timeless reality of Ideas, and finally Book 4 intensifies Schopenhauer's pessimistic view of the ordinary life of desire and action, and advocates an abolition of the will within oneself as the path to what is ethically good, and ultimately to a kind of resigned mystical salvation.

Representation

In its first aspect, then, the world is representation. The world, in other words, is what presents itself in a subject's experience. (A more old-fashioned translation of the German *Vorstellung* gives us 'the world as idea' – but to retain this could be misleading because of Schopenhauer's use of *Idee* for a Platonic Idea elsewhere in the system.) Schopenhauer begins by expounding an idealist position. This is the view that the material objects which we experience depend for their order and their existence on the knowing subject. He calls his position transcendental idealism, which is Kant's term, but he also emphasizes his continuity with Berkeley, as he sees in the latter's doctrine that 'to be is to be perceived' the initial glimmer of the truth in idealism – Kant's contribution being to explain how what is perceived constitutes a world of objects when it is governed by the necessary rules of space, time, and causality. Schopenhauer's account of the world of empirical things is what it was in *The Fourfold Root:* empirical things consist of matter, which fills distinct portions of space and time, and which is in causal interaction with other such portions. But his idealism says that without the subject of experience, all such objects would not exist.

To be more specific, it is *individual* things that would not exist without the experiencing subject. What we experience in the ordinary course of our lives are distinct things. One table is an individual distinct from another, one animal or person likewise. But what is the principle on which this division of the world into individual things works? Schopenhauer has a very clear and plausible answer: location in space and time. Two tables are distinct individuals because they occupy distinct portions of space, or of time, or of both. Now if you take this view, and also think, with Kant, that the organizing of things under the structure of space and time stems from the subject, and applies only to the world of phenomena, not to the world as it is in itself, then you will conclude that individuals do not exist in the world as it is in itself. The world would not be broken up into individual things, if it were not for the space and time which we, as subjects, impose. Here then are two important tenets of Schopenhauer's philosophy. Space and time are the principle of individuation, or in his favoured Latin version, the *principium individuationis*; and there can be no individuals on the 'in itself' side of the line.

Schopenhauer has four main arguments for idealism. One alleges that we cannot imagine anything which exists outside our own minds, because 'what we are imagining at that moment is . . . nothing but just the process in the intellect of a knowing being' (*W2*, 5). This is reminiscent of a controversial argument attempted by Berkeley, who thought that an unperceived tree could not be imagined. Schopenhauer's use of the argument is not very convincing, however, because even though *my imagining* a world independent of my mind does presuppose my own mind, the existence of what I imagine – a world independent of my mind – does not. A second argument is the claim that idealism is the only viable alternative to scepticism. Scepticism maintains that we can have no certain knowledge about the existence or nature of material things, because all that we can be certain of is what falls within our own consciousness. If you deny idealism (the argument runs) and think that the world of material things has to exist wholly outside a subject's consciousness, then you will have to admit that scepticism wins the day, and that we can never have certain knowledge about a world of material things. If we wish to preserve our entitlement to *knowledge* concerning the world of things that occupy space and time and follow causal laws, the solution is to accept that they do not lie outside our consciousness.

Schopenhauer's third argument adds to this by suggesting that realism – the alternative to idealism – saddles itself with two 'worlds', one of which is redundant:

> According to realism, the world is supposed to exist, as we know it, independently of this knowledge. Now let us once remove from it all knowing beings, and thus leave behind only inorganic and vegetable nature. Rock, tree, and brook are there, and the blue sky . . . But then let us subsequently put into the world a knowing being. That world then presents itself *once more* in his brain . . . Thus to the *first* world a *second* has been added, which, although completely separated from the first, resembles it to a nicety . . . . All this proves absurd enough, and thus

30

leads to the conviction that that absolutely *objective* world outside the head, independent of it and *prior* to all knowledge, which we at first imagined we had conceived, was already no other than the second world already known *subjectively*, the world of the representation, and that it is this alone which we are actually capable of conceiving. (*W*2, 9–10)

Schopenhauer is here in a territory littered both before and after him with debates of some complexity. The three arguments so far discussed can be found already in Berkeley. They are, however, not decisive for quite simple reasons. The realist may reply to the 'scepticism' argument by saying that if the choice is between scepticism and idealism, then scepticism is the better option. The idea that material things depend on the subject for their existence may seem too high a price to pay for a guarantee of knowledge. Also the argument only says that if we can have any certain knowledge, idealism must be preferred. One might settle for not having certain knowledge, and insist that the empirical world must nevertheless be conceived as existing independently of the subject's consciousness. To the third argument, that the world of things existing outside consciousness is redundant, the realist can reply simply that this world outside consciousness would be *the* world. It is only the idealist who wants to say that the *picture* of material things which we have in consciousness is already a world of material things. The realist does not accept this, and makes a clear distinction between the one world existing independently of us and our picture of it. However, Schopenhauer's points correspond to familiar parts of the debate, and are valuable against some opponents. A realism which said both that we can be certain only about what lies within consciousness, and that the world outside consciousness exactly resembles the picture we have built of it, would be threatened by his criticisms.

The fourth argument for idealism is the one which Schopenhauer most relies on. It rests on the concepts *subject* and *object*. The subject is that which knows or experiences, the object that which is known or experienced. The world of representation, for Schopenhauer, requires

31

both. He makes two large claims: first, that nothing can be both object and subject; secondly that there can never be a subject without an object, or an object without a subject. It is the last point which he takes to establish idealism, and indeed to make it something obvious. Nothing can be an object for experience without there being a subject to experience it or think about it. But why must we think of material objects in space and time in this way? Schopenhauer would argue that the point of calling them objects is to indicate that they can and do fall within our experience. But then he also requires us to believe that whatever we can experience must exist only in relation to our experiencing it. This simple principle is central to Schopenhauer's position. Because of it, he does not think that idealism can be seriously doubted, once one properly understands it. But it is surely a questionable principle.

A fair proportion of Book I of *The World as Will and Representation* is devoted to the distinction between perception and conceptual reasoning. As we saw in the previous chapter, Schopenhauer thinks that we share our perceptual abilities with other animals, but that concepts and reasoning are what mark us out from them. Perceiving the world is the business of what he calls intellect or understanding, and he suggests that conceptual thinking and judgement play no part in this. On the other hand, manipulating concepts to form judgements, relating judgements to one another as premiss and conclusion, and so on, is the business of what he calls reason. By playing down the significance of reason and treating concepts as more or less faint abstractions out of direct experience or intuition, Schopenhauer paves the way for a close assimilation between the human mind and that of other living creatures.

Will

As we cross from the First Book into the Second, a sudden reversal takes place. This focuses on a key question. In the world as representation, what am I? The world spreads out before me, containing individual material things in space and time which change according to causal laws - but I myself am just the subject which is distinct from every object that it experiences, including that object which I call my body. Something is missing. I seem to be 'a winged cherub without a body' (W1, 99), the world confronting me as something alien to which I do not belong.

> For the purely knowing subject as such, this body is a representation like any other, an object among objects. Its movements and actions are so far known to him in just the same way as the changes of all other objects of perception; and they would be equally strange and incomprehensible to him, if their meaning were not unravelled for him in an entirely different way. Otherwise, he would see his conduct follow on presented motives with the constancy of a law of nature, just as the changes of other objects follow upon causes, stimuli, and motives. But he would be no nearer to understanding the influence of the motives than he is to understanding the connexion with its cause of any other effect that appears before him. (W1, 99-100)

Schopenhauer is generating a puzzlement in order to make us receptive to the central idea of the whole book, which is now unveiled:

> All this, however, is not the case; on the contrary, the answer to the riddle is given to the subject of knowledge appearing as an individual, and this answer is given in the word *will*. This and this alone gives him the key to his own phenomenon, reveals to him the significance and shows him the inner mechanism of his being, his actions, his movements. To the subject of knowing, who appears as an individual only through his identity with the body, this body is given in two entirely different ways. It is given in perception of the intellect as representation, as an object among objects, liable to the laws of these objects. But it is also given in a quite different way, namely as what is known immediately to everyone, and is denoted by the word *will*. (W1, 100)

33

What Schopenhauer means is that when I act (when I do something) my body moves; and my awareness of its movement is unlike my awareness of other events that I perceive. I am 'outside' other objects, or they are 'outside' me – but my own body is mine in a uniquely intimate way. This can be expressed by saying that other events are merely observed to happen, whereas movements of my body are expressions of *my will*. Schopenhauer's account of acts of will is anti-dualist. A dualist would maintain that the mental realm and the bodily realm are distinct, and that *willing* (or volition) was an event in the mental realm, while the movement of the body was something distinct that occurred in the physical realm. Schopenhauer denies this:

> The act of will and the action of the body are not two different states objectively known, connected by the bond of causality; they do not stand in the relation of cause and effect, but are one and the same thing, though given in two entirely different ways, first quite directly, and then in perception for the understanding. (ibid.)

Wanting, striving, and trying are to be seen as things that we do with our bodies, not as events that occur in detachment from our bodies. They manifest themselves in physical reality, but also retain an 'inner' aspect, because each of us knows what he or she strives for, in a direct, non-observational way. Thus what Schopenhauer calls the 'action of the body' is neither in a wholly mental or a wholly physical realm, but is one single occurrence which presents two aspects: we each have 'inner' awareness of something that is also part of the ordinary empirical world, and can be observed as such.

This account of acts of will is a decisive step for Schopenhauer, since it places the human subject firmly within the material world. If striving towards ends is setting the body in motion, then, while we will, we are rooted in the world of objects. Schopenhauer thus cannot conceive of a subject of will as being anything other than bodily. He also makes the converse claim that our bodily existence is nothing other than willing.

Whenever we undergo feelings of fear or desire, attraction or repulsion, whenever the body itself behaves according to the various unconscious functions of nourishment, reproduction, or survival, Schopenhauer discerns will manifesting itself – but in a new and extended sense. What he wants to show is that ordinary conscious willing is no different in its basic nature from the many other processes which set the body, or parts of it, in motion. Admittedly, willing to act involves conscious thinking – it involves the body's being caused to move by motives in the intellect – but it is, for Schopenhauer, not different in principle from the beating of the heart, the activation of the saliva glands, or the arousal of the sexual organs. All can be seen as an individual organism manifesting will, in Schopenhauer's sense. The body itself is will; more specifically, it is a manifestation of will to life (*Wille zum Leben*), a kind of blind striving, at a level beneath that of conscious thought and action, which is directed towards the preservation of life, and towards engendering life anew.

This interesting idea is wrapped up in the much wider claim that the whole world in itself is will. Just as my body's movements have an inner aspect not revealed in objective experience, so does the rest of the world. Schopenhauer seeks an account which makes all fundamental forces in nature homogeneous, and thinks that science is inherently unsatisfying because it always tails off without explaining the essence or hidden inner character of the phenomena whose behaviour it accounts for. His unifying account of nature is that all natural processes are a manifestation of will. This is likely at first sight to be dismissed as fanciful – but we should heed Schopenhauer's warning that he is vastly extending the concept 'will':

> hitherto the identity of the inner essence of any striving and operating force in nature with the will has not been recognized, and therefore the many kinds of phenomena that are only different species of the same genus were not regarded as such . . . Consequently, no word could exist to denote the concept of this genus. I therefore name the genus after its

most important species, the direct knowledge of which lies nearest to us, and leads to the indirect knowledge of all the others. But anyone who is incapable of carrying out the required extension of the concept will remain involved in a permanent misunderstanding. (*W1*, 111)

So we must not transfer 'will' simple-mindedly from human actions to the whole of nature. It serves only as the most convenient term where none yet exists. Nevertheless, this aspect of Schopenhauer's philosophy is puzzling. What is the 'required extension' of the concept? Perhaps it is an extension of sense: if 'will' is now to have a new meaning, this might save Schopenhauer from claiming something ridiculous. But this line should not be taken too far. Schopenhauer insists that 'will' is not interchangeable with 'force', for example (*W1*, 111–12), and that the issue is not a mere 'dispute about words'. In saying that all processes are will, 'we have in fact referred something more unknown to something infinitely better known, indeed to the one thing really known to us immediately and completely' (*W1*, 112). To subsume willing under force (or energy, which has also been suggested) is not Schopenhauer's intention. The global doctrine of will can tell us something informative only because we have some grasp of what willing is from our own actions. An alternative interpretation is that Schopenhauer is keeping the sense of 'will' fixed, and simply widening the range of phenomena that it refers to. He does say that in mechanics '*seeking* shows itself as gravitation, . . . *fleeing* as reception of motion' and similar things (*W2*, 298); he is prepared to speak in remarkable terms of 'the powerful, irresistible impulse with which masses of water rush downwards, the persistence and determination with which the magnet always turns back to the North Pole, the keen desire with which iron flies to the magnet' (*W1*, 117–18). How are we to take this? If meant literally, it is merely embarrassing. But perhaps he is doing something more subtle here, and attempting to teach us our own kinship with nature by rhetorical means: the behaviour of the inorganic world is to an extent '*like* the vehemence of human desires' and so 'it will not cost us a great effort of the imagination to recognize once more our own inner nature, even at so great a distance'. This is not to say that iron really desires anything, or that water rushes because it wants to.

What we usually call willing is supposed to be a clear guide to the way the world is. So 'will' must still be understood in terms of its application to human actions; however, we must enlarge its sense at least far enough to avoid the barbarity of thinking that every process in the world has a mind, a consciousness, or a purpose behind it. For the most part, Schopenhauer assures us, the world operates blindly and 'in a dull, one-sided, and unalterable manner' – and the same is even true of many manifestations of the will within each human individual. The following passage states Schopenhauer's view as clearly as any:

> only the *will* is *thing in itself* . . . It is that of which all representation, all object, is the phenomenon, the visibility, the *objectivity*. It is the innermost essence, the kernel, of every particular thing and also of the whole. It appears in every blindly acting force of nature, and also in the deliberate conduct of man, and the great difference between the two concerns only the degree of the manifestation, not the inner nature of what is manifested. (*W1*, 110)

This surely means that every force in nature, those that involve conscious purpose and those that do not, must be understood as some form of striving or end-seeking, even if in highly attenuated form.

Two more peculiarities of this doctrine should be noted. First, if the will is the thing in itself, it is not something occupying space and time. Space and time are merely the subject-imposed structure of the world as representation, and the thing in itself is what remains when the world as representation is thought away. Given Schopenhauer's idea that space and time are the principle of individuation, the thing in itself cannot be split up into separate individuals. Beyond representation, space, and time, it is simply the world as a whole that is to be conceived as will. Secondly, there can be no causal interaction between the will, as

Die Welt

als

Wille und Vorstellung.

Von

Arthur Schopenhauer.

Dritte, verbesserte und beträchtlich vermehrte Auflage.

Erster Band.

Vier Bücher, nebst einem Anhange, der die Kritik der Kantischen
Philosophie enthält.

Ob nicht Natur zuletzt sich doch ergründe?
Goethe.

Leipzig:

F. A. Brockhaus.

1859.

6. Title page of *The World as Will and Representation*

thing in itself, and events in the ordinary empirical world. Causality too is something which operates only at the level of empirical changes occurring to individual material things, not at the level of the thing in itself. Kant seemed to require that the thing in itself could impinge upon us causally, rather like some empirical object, and Schopenhauer was well aware that this claim was the stumbling-block of Kantianism for many of his contemporaries. Schopenhauer himself avoids the problem, and never claims that the will as thing in itself is a cause. But then what is the relationship between the world in itself and the things and events that lie within our empirical knowledge? Schopenhauer talks sometimes of the will's 'manifestation' in empirical reality, but his preferred term is 'objectification'. This means just that the world shows to us the side of it which we can experience. We have to think of the single will and its objectification in a multitude of phenomena as two sides of a coin, two aspects of the same world.

A big problem here concerns the knowability of the thing in itself. Schopenhauer's doctrine of the will is metaphysical. Metaphysics, for him, gives an account of the fundamental nature of reality, but uses the data of experience as the only possible guide: 'the solution to the riddle of the world must come from an understanding of the world itself . . . the task of metaphysics is not to pass over experience in which the world exists, but to understand it thoroughly, since inner and outer experience are certainly the principal source of all knowledge' (W1, 428). Strictly speaking, our knowledge reaches only as far as the phenomena of inner and outer experience. So we do not – cannot – know the bare thing in itself. When I am conscious of my own willing in action, what I know is a phenomenal manifestation of the will, not the thing in itself. Nevertheless, it is this knowledge of my own willing which is to provide the key to knowing the nature of the whole world in itself. How?

As we saw, Schopenhauer sets up a contrast between experience of the world of material objects and 'immediate' awareness of one's own willing. Sometimes he writes as if the latter amounted to knowledge of the thing in itself directly: 'my body is the only object of which I know not merely the one side, that of the representation, but also the other, that is called *will*' (W1, 125); 'Everyone finds himself to be this will, in which the inner nature of the world consists' (W1, 162); 'a way *from within* stands open to us to that real inner nature of things to which we cannot penetrate *from without*' (W2, 195). This may suggest direct cognitive contact with the thing in itself inside us, and a further inference that everything in the world has a similar inner nature. But we must wonder how this can be achieved, if the thing in itself is strictly unknowable. When he is being more careful, Schopenhauer says that even the act of will which we know 'immediately' is an event in time, and is therefore part of our representation, rather than the thing in itself. Still, he says, the thing in itself, though it 'does not appear quite naked', has 'to a great extent cast off its veils' in our 'inner' awareness of action (W2, 197). In consciousness of our own willing we are still on this side of the divide between representation and thing in itself, but we can say that we come closer to knowledge of the thing in itself. This is still troubling, however. If knowledge of our acts of will is the nearest we get to the thing in itself, and if even here we do not know it directly, what grounds do we really have for claiming to know what it is?

As an exercise in metaphysics, Schopenhauer's doctrine of the will as thing in itself is so obviously flawed that some people have doubted whether he really means it – perhaps *will* is just a concept which explains a wide range of phenomena, and is not supposed to extend to the unknowable thing in itself? On the other hand, if that were the whole of his position, he could offer no 'solution to the riddle' in the way that he clearly intends. Given such problems, it is perhaps not surprising that his metaphysics has had few followers. Nevertheless, to stop there would be short-sighted. Schopenhauer's more restricted notion of the *will to life*, which characterizes observable aspects of human and animal behaviour, is an interesting and powerful idea. His conception of will expressing itself within humanity, and the polarity he discovers between our being governed by the will and our escaping it, enables him, as we shall see, to present large tracts of our lives in a new light. It enables him to explain thought-processes as having an organic, survival-directed function, to show the influence of unconscious drives and feelings on the intellect, to suggest that our picture of ourselves as rational individual thinkers is in some sense an illusion, to place sexuality at the core of human psychology, to account for the power of music and the value of aesthetic experience, to argue that ordinary life is inevitably unfulfilled, and to advocate the renunciation of individual desires as the route to reconciliation with our existence. It has been these applications, rather than the bald metaphysical statement that the thing in itself is will, that have had the most influence on philosophers, psychologists, and artists of later generations.

Chapter 4
Will, body, and the self

Unity of body and will

Schopenhauer's claim 'My body and my will are one' (*W1*, 102) has a
number of different aspects to it. The first, as we saw, is the idea that
acts of will are movements of the body. Schopenhauer takes a robust
line on this, saying that 'every true, genuine, immediate act of the
will is also at once and directly a manifest act of the body' (*W1*, 101).
This would suggest, somewhat perversely, that there can be no such
thing as a willing which goes unfulfilled because one's muscles or
nerves do not function in the right way. (Would Schopenhauer say
that stroke victims have not 'genuinely' willed, if their bodies fail to
move as they want them to?) But Schopenhauer is trying to oust the
traditional division between mental and physical, and to supplant it
with a division between will on the one hand and intellect and reason
on the other. Perception, judgement, and reasoning are all functions
of what he has called representation. We observe the way a state of
affairs is in the world of objects, judge that it should be altered or
preserved, and form the intention to act. Schopenhauer's chief point
is that none of this is yet *willing*. The operations of perception,
thought, and intention are quite separate preparatory events
which may trigger the will – the body, that is – into action. He
plays down the gap between willing and the movements one carries
out with one's body, concentrating instead on the gulf between

representing the world of objects, and being in goal-seeking motion within it.

Schopenhauer's other evidence for the unity of will and the body is that almost everything that impinges on the body sets off some reaction of the will, and that conversely, when the will is aroused, there are always bodily manifestations. The list of mental states included under the heading of the will is extensive:

> all desiring, striving, wishing, demanding, longing, hoping, loving, rejoicing, jubilation, and the like, no less than not willing or resisting, all abhorring, fleeing, fearing, being angry, hating, mourning, suffering pains – in short, all emotions and passions. For these emotions and passions are weaker or stronger, violent and stormy or else quiet impulses of one's own will, which is either restrained or unleashed, satisfied or unsatisfied. In their many variations they relate to the successful or frustrated attainment of that which is willed, to the endurance or the overcoming of that which is abhorred. Consequently, they are explicit affections of the same will which is active in decisions and actions. (F, 11)

Sometimes, Schopenhauer admits, when the bodily senses are affected our reaction is neutral, and does not rouse the will in any of these ways – but only rarely. For the most part, such an occurrence is to some degree painful or pleasant, welcome or irritating. Similarly, when we are in one of the mental states on Schopenhauer's list, there is usually a characteristic bodily accompaniment: the heart beats faster, the blood drains from our face or suffuses it. Thus 'every vehement and excessive movement of the will, in other words, every emotion, agitates the body and its inner workings directly and immediately' (W1, 101). For Schopenhauer these considerations tend to show the identity of the body with the will. They do at least suggest a close affinity between bodily existence and the empirical manifestations of willing in Schopenhauer's broader sense.

A representation in the conscious mind which causes the body to move in action is what Schopenhauer calls a *motive*. We share some kinds of motive with other animals that perceive the world. For example, behaviour in a cat which is caused by perceiving a predator or some food would be classed by Schopenhauer as willing brought about by a motive. Humans, on the other hand, are distinctive in being able to act not just on perceptual motives, but also on rational ones: representing matters conceptually, we reason ourselves to a conclusion about what to do, and this process plays a causal role in setting us into action. A cat may eat because it senses food and is hungry, a human being because doing so is judged the best course of action. But willing manifests itself in the body's movements in the same way in both cases. Different kinds of willing really differ, for Schopenhauer, only in the causes that precede them. He makes a basic distinction between three kinds of cause. These are motive, stimulus, and cause pure and simple (as found in mechanical and chemical changes).

So far 'willing' has stood for a range of mental states which have bodily manifestations, including active striving, the emotions, and feelings of pleasure and pain. But some manifestations of the will in the body are not what we should call mental states at all, and are of a kind which we share even with lowlier parts of nature. Plants behave in certain ways in reaction to light, moisture, gravity, and so on. They do not perform actions, and their movements and modifications are not caused by motives, for the simple reason that they have no minds with which to perceive. The plant's turning towards the sun is caused by a *stimulus*, rather than by a motive. Nevertheless, Schopenhauer is prepared to call such plant-behaviour a manifestation of will, because he thinks it can only be understood as goal-directed, even if there is no mind present to entertain the goal. Having located will in bodily movement, and distinguished it from representation, he sees an affinity between the plant's movement in response to stimuli and those of the cat and the human brought about by motives. It is clear that human beings and animals also respond to stimuli – the involuntary contraction of the pupil of the eye provides but one example. This occurrence, for Schopenhauer, is equally a manifestation of the will – though not an *act* of will, because it is not caused by a conscious representation of the world.

Will to life

Schopenhauer's conception of the will is not restricted to the body's episodic reactions to motives and stimuli, for he claims that 'the whole body is nothing but the objectified will' (*W1*, 100), meaning that the way in which the body grows and develops, and the way in which its parts are organized, reveal a principle of striving towards ends which is 'blindly' at work:

> Teeth, gullet, and intestinal canal are objectified hunger; the genitals are objectified sexual impulse; grasping hands and nimble feet correspond to the more indirect strivings of the will which they represent. (*W1*, 108)

What underlies and explains the body's functioning, indeed its very existence, is its being directed towards life – or what Schopenhauer calls its *will to life*. (The usual translation of *Wille zum Leben* as 'will to live' is linguistically correct, but what Schopenhauer has in mind is more inclusive; it is a striving not just to live, but also to engender life and to protect offspring. [See *W2*, 484–5.] In other words, *life*, rather than *living*, is the common end of all *Wille zum Leben*.) Schopenhauer is boldly seeking a single hypothesis to explain the ways in which all life-forms grow, function, and behave.

It is easy to think that the idea of the 'will to life' is wrongly fixated on the idea that there are purposes in nature. However, although Schopenhauer speaks of 'purposes' or 'ends' being fulfilled by behaviour patterns and the workings of particular organs, he clearly does not think that organisms entertain any conscious purposes – for the will works 'blindly':

we see at once from the instinct and mechanical skill of animals that the will is also active where it is not guided by any knowledge . . . The one-year-old bird has no notion of the eggs for which it builds a nest; the young spider has no idea of the prey for which it spins a web; the ant-lion has no notion of the ant for which it digs a cavity for the first time. . . . Even in us the same will in many ways acts blindly; as in all those functions of our body which are not guided by knowledge, in all its vital and vegetative processes, digestion, circulation, secretion, growth, and reproduction. (W1, 114–15)

So, despite superficial appearances, Schopenhauer does not simply wish to understand nature in anthropomorphic terms. Although he asks us to interpret the world using concepts applied first to ourselves, the notion of the will to life has the effect of demoting humanity from any special status separate from the rest of nature. First, in our bodies, the same 'blind' force operates as throughout nature: we are organized to live and to propagate life not by any conscious act of will. Secondly, there is a close continuity between even the conscious, purposive willing of human action and the life-preserving functions and instincts at work elsewhere. In our seeking of mates and providing for offspring, we are driven by the same instincts as other animals. And Schopenhauer sees the human capacities for perception, rationality, and action as an offshoot of the same wider principle which leads insects to build nests, feathers to grow, and cells to divide. In this respect, the will to life can seem quite a forward-looking notion. Another crucial feature is Schopenhauer's steadfast opposition to anything approaching an external or divine purpose for nature. Even though it is 'a single will' which expresses itself throughout the multiplicity of phenomena, this means only that all behaviour is of the same striving or goal-directed kind. All life-forms strive towards life; but there is no coordinated purpose to nature, rather the kind of purposelessness and conflict which are usually associated with Darwinism. Schopenhauer derides those 'pantheists' and 'Spinozists' who think the world divine, but have not 'the remotest idea why the whole tragi-comedy exists' (W2, 357).

On the other hand, Schopenhauer does believe that the various species of animate and inanimate things in the world are eternal and static. There are not only individuals, which we happen to classify as ants, or oak trees, or magnetic fields. Rather, each individual is of a *kind*, and the kinds that can exist are fixed. Thus, while individual things come and go over time, *the ant* or *the oak tree*, as a kind, is a permanent feature of empirical reality. Schopenhauer has two ways of expressing this point, which he frequently repeats. One is to say that the will (the thing in itself) manifests or objectifies itself in a series of *grades*. The other is to say that *the ant* and *the oak tree* as such are Ideas, or as he often puts it '(Platonic) Ideas'. The most adequately objective knowledge we could have would be of the nature of these abiding forms 'fixed in the nature of things'. Such objective knowledge would not consist in knowing the thing in itself in its naked form, which is impossible, but in knowing the timeless patterns of the things that are experienceable by us.

The following passage shows quite well how Schopenhauer uses his doctrine of the will to life and his notion of the order of Ideas in nature:

> everywhere in nature we see contest, struggle, and the fluctuation of victory . . . Every grade of the will's objectification fights for the matter, the space, and the time of another . . . This universal conflict is to be seen most clearly in the animal kingdom. Animals have the vegetable kingdom for their nourishment, and within the animal kingdom again every animal is the prey and food of some other. This means that the matter in which an animal's Idea manifests itself must stand aside for the manifestation of another Idea, since every animal can maintain its own existence only by the incessant elimination of another's. Thus the will to life generally feasts on itself, and is in different forms its own nourishment, till finally the human race, because it subdues all the others, regards nature as manufactured for its own use. (*W*1, 146–7)

Intellect as an outgrowth of will

Now we come to a step in Schopenhauer's argument whose importance cannot be overestimated. He claims that all our knowledge of the empirical world is the product of the kind of organism we are. The structure of knowledge and of its objects depends on the kind of manifestation of will to life which its subject happens to be. Everything the reader was told at the outset about the world of representation, the forms of space, time, and causality which govern the objects of our experience, and the concepts and judgements which we can obtain from them by abstraction – all of this is merely a surface beneath which lurks the driving force of our nature, the will. We grow into creatures who can perceive, judge, and reason, in order to fulfil the ends of life: survival, nourishment, and reproduction. In Schopenhauer's narrative this is a marked change of fortune for the human subject. The capacity for knowledge on which we pride ourselves suddenly appears as merely a way in which a particular species manipulates the environment that impinges on it, so as to foster its well-being:

> [the intellect] is designed for comprehending those ends on the attainment of which depend individual life and its propagation. But such an intellect is by no means destined to interpret the inner essence-in-itself of things and of the world, which exists independently of the knower. (W2, 284)

To establish this picture, Schopenhauer has to claim not only that all biological functions are manifestations of will to life, but also that knowledge, perception, and reasoning are biological functions. This he does by espousing a particularly blunt form of materialism: states of mind are states of the brain. If, instead of regarding our processes of thought and perception from the point of view of self-consciousness, we take an 'objective' view of them, we must conclude them to be 'nothing more than the physiological function of an internal organ, the brain' (W2, 273). The whole world of individual objects in space and time consists only of our representations, and representations are brain-functions. So the brain, the 'pulpy mass in the skull', supports the whole world of objects – Schopenhauer's materialist account of mental states combines with his idealism to produce the claim that the empirical world of individual things is a product of the brain's functioning. For fear of saying such things, people in the past invented the notion of an immaterial soul, but Schopenhauer will have none of that:

> We say fearlessly that this pulpy mass, like every vegetable or animal part, is also an organic structure, like all its humbler relations in the inferior dwelling-place of our irrational brothers' heads, down to the humblest that scarcely apprehends. (W2, 273)

Finally, the brain is a biological organ, and so it cannot be exempt from Schopenhauer's doctrine of the will to life:

> the *will-to-know*, objectively perceived, is the brain, just as the *will-to-walk*, objectively perceived, is the foot; the *will-to-grasp*, the hand; the *will-to-digest*, the stomach; the *will-to-procreate*, the genitals, and so on. (W2, 259)

So the position is this: our capacity for knowledge of empirical objects resides in the functioning of the brain, the brain is an organ of the body, and all organs of the body have developed in order to propagate life. Our much-vaunted knowledge is thus a derivative feature of what we are; the primary element in us is the will that manifests itself in the body as a whole. Conscious actions, caused by perception of the world and reasoning about it, are merely one way in which this will in our bodies is set into motion. The individual human subject is different from other kinds of striving thing in the world only by virtue of the fact that the particular organization of his or her brain gives rise to self-consciousness and reasoning. But these capacities are only the tip of an iceberg, whose bulk is the will. Our predicament is to be driven by this will, whether we like it or not, into conflict, pain, and frustration. Schopenhauer still holds out the hope of rising above this predicament, but, as we shall see, the will within us must be suspended or turn against itself before we can exploit the capacities of our intellects to their full potential. Knowledge must eventually 'throw off its yoke, and, free from all the aims of the will, exist purely for itself, simply as a clear mirror of the world' (*W1*, 152). But for that to happen is very much an exception.

The self

What am I? Schopenhauer can say that I am an individual item in the world, a living, bodily thing of a certain species, which is capable of self-conscious thought and action. But he makes it something of a puzzle how I can think of myself in this way. In his philosophy the self is seen successively as a subject of experience and knowledge, a subject of will and action, a bodily manifestation of will to life, and a pure mirror of timeless reality. Sometimes it is as if a struggle for dominance is being waged between these different conceptions. The dichotomy between *subject* and *object*, which is the starting-point for the whole of *The World as Will and Representation*, is especially important here. As we saw, he explains that the subject is that which knows, the object that which is known by it. But this must leave us in some doubt about what a subject is.

A subject of representation is, for Schopenhauer, a single consciousness in which many diverse experiences of objects are united. Material things and conceptual thoughts are representations for the subject. But the subject itself is the 'I' that thinks and perceives, as opposed to the things thought and the things perceived. It is vital to understand that Schopenhauer's subject of representations is not any part of the world of objects. It is not a thing at all. It is not in space or time, does not interact causally with objects, is not visible, not identified with the body, or even with the individual human being. His favourite metaphorical images for it are the eye that looks out on the world but cannot see itself, and the extensionless point at which light-rays focus in a concave mirror. The subject is where experiences all converge, but it is never itself an object of experience: 'We never know it, but it is precisely that which knows wherever there is knowledge' (W1, 5). Schopenhauer is not alone in having such a view of the subject. It is recognizable as a version of Kant's conception of the pure 'I' of self-consciousness (apperception); moreover, says Schopenhauer, 'the fine passage from the sacred *Upanishad* applies: "It is not to be seen: it sees everything; it is not to be heard: it hears everything; it is not to be recognized: it recognizes everything"' (R, 208). Wittgenstein later borrowed Schopenhauer's image of the eye that cannot see itself and the idea that the subject was not part of the world.

Schopenhauer's attitude to this pure subject of representation is ambivalent. On the one hand, he says that 'Everyone finds himself as this subject' (W1, 5). We are conscious not only of what we think and perceive, but of *being* that which thinks and perceives; moreover, he suggests, we cannot avoid the idea that that which thinks and perceives is distinct from every object of which it is conscious – even the body, which is 'an object among objects'. At the same time, however, each of us is an individual distinct from others. Each of us is closely associated with one particular part of the material world, and, as a subject of action or will, each of us must be a bodily thing. We seem to be two kinds of subject at once: subject of willing, which is essentially embodied, and subject of knowledge, which knows everything objectively, including its own body and acts of will, and hovers outside the world of individual things altogether. Our conception of ourselves ought, perhaps, to be split. Yet we think of the 'I' that thinks and perceives and the 'I' that acts as one and the same. Schopenhauer calls this a 'miracle *par excellence*', saying that 'the identity of the subject of willing with that of knowing by virtue whereof . . . the word "I" includes and indicates both, is the knot of the world, and hence inexplicable' (R, 211–12).

One may think that Schopenhauer inadvertently refutes his own conception of the pure subject which is not an object. For he admits that it provides at best an incomplete and perplexing way of thinking of oneself, says that it is inexplicable how 'I' could refer both to this pure subject and to the acting, material body, and even has to invoke the notion of a 'miracle' to get round the problem. We may also not be convinced that we do 'find ourselves' as the pure knowing subject, or that this is a conception which a philosophical account of self-consciousness needs to use at all. However, Schopenhauer's difficulties are not simply a matter of ineptness on his part – they go deep into an area of enduring perplexity. Each of us is not *merely* an object in the world; some account needs to be given of one's awareness of being oneself, of being 'inside' one's experience and seeming to be distinct from the rest of the world. Schopenhauer is not a dualist: he eschews any notion that souls, spirits, or immaterial substances constitute part of reality. Reality is material, and what each of us refers to using 'I' is, partly, an active, material thing in the world. But he is surely right in saying that that cannot be the end of the story. It seems true that I somehow 'find myself as a subject', however precisely we account for that. Some philosophers more recently have suggested that there is a fundamental, perhaps insuperable problem in trying to square 'subjective' and 'objective' views of ourselves. The underlying difficulty which Schopenhauer reveals is a substantial philosophical issue.

The struggle between competing views of the self is made even more intense by Schopenhauer's materialist account of the workings of the intellect as brain-functions, and his doctrine that the individual's body is an expression of will-to-life.

> That which in self-consciousness, and hence subjectively, is the intellect, presents itself in the consciousness of other things, and hence objectively, as the brain; and that which in self-consciousness, and hence subjectively, is the will, presents itself in the consciousness of other things, and hence objectively, as the entire organism. (*W2*, 245)

That focus of brain-activity (or the subject of knowledge) is indeed, as an indivisible point, simple, yet it is not on that account a substance (soul), but a mere condition or state ... This *knowing* and conscious *ego* is related to the will, which is the basis of its phenomenal appearance, as the image in the focus of the concave mirror is to that mirror itself; and, like that image, it has only a conditioned, in fact, properly speaking, a merely apparent reality. Far from being the absolutely first thing (as Fichte taught, for example), it is at bottom tertiary, since it presupposes the organism, and the organism presupposes the will. (*W2*, 278)

We need to tease out two distinct elements here. One is Schopenhauer's materialism, the other his view that the will is our essence.

We can consider ourselves both subjectively and objectively. If we are considering ourselves objectively, as things occurring in the empirical world, then materialism is the most plausible and consistent position to take, according to Schopenhauer. To be a materialist pure and simple would be 'one-sided' (*W2*, 13), because materialism can never give a proper account of what it is to be a subject who experiences and understands the world: 'materialism is the philosophy of the subject that forgets to take account of itself'. But one side of the truth is an objective account of ourselves as things inhabiting the empirical world, and the only choice here is to conceive of ourselves as material occupants of space and time, falling under causal laws. So what from one viewpoint we call thought and perception are, from the other viewpoint, processes of the material brain and nervous system. From this objective point of view, the subject which we take ourselves to be is – in Schopenhauer's most extreme claim about it – 'merely apparent'.

But even this unsettled combination of subjective and objective views about oneself is not the complete predicament which Schopenhauer places us in. For brain and organism are not merely part of an inert, material reality. They are expressions of the blind will in nature, enabling

53

life to exist and propagate itself. The will is primary, and lies beneath the division between subject and object altogether. The larger contrast between will and representation reasserts itself here. The subject that represents and the object that is represented are both, in a sense, illusory, because in the world in itself the division between subject and object does not exist. Even if I the subject disappeared, and along with me all the individual objects that make up my experience, the will would still be there in itself, continuing to strive and throw up new life-forms. And the most fundamental point about the self, for Schopenhauer, is that this same will is exactly what now strives away within the bodily organism that has produced me the subject.

Chapter 5
Character, sex, and the unconscious

Will and intellect

For Schopenhauer, the primary element in human beings is the will. The intellect is only secondary; Schopenhauer explains it as a particular manifestation of the will to life in the brain and nervous system, and 'a mere tool in the service of the will' (*W2*, 205). Schopenhauer invents many images for the relationship between intellect and will, but his favourite is that of the sighted, lame man who is carried on the shoulders of the strong, blind man. The intellect is conscious, and is our window on the world, but the driving force which takes us where we are going is deeper down inside the psyche, inside the body or organism which we also are. The doctrine of the primacy of the will has many applications which are broadly psychological or ethical. Schopenhauer is in some respects a forerunner of twentieth-century views about the unconscious mind and the influence of sexuality on our behaviour, both of which emerge from his considerations of the opposition between intellect and will. His ethics also depends on the idea that the core of each individual, which makes them the person they are, is not the intellect, but the enduring, underlying will.

Once again we find that the individual's sense of his or her identity is something of a precarious affair. The self is a kind of compound between the will and the intellect. Although objectively the intellect is

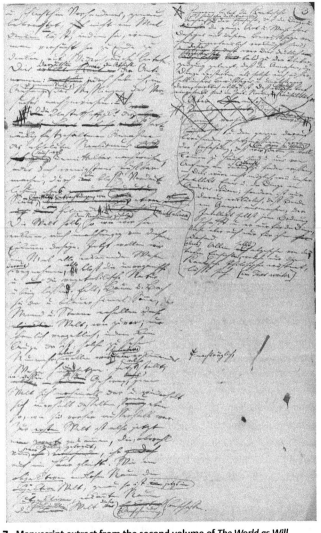

7. Manuscript extract from the second volume of *The World as Will and Representation*

an expression of will as well, in our own self-consciousness we can distinguish the intellect as that part of us which is occupied with conscious perception and thought. The subjective symptoms of this split are various kinds of conflict and domination of which we may be aware: a 'strange interplay within us' between the intellect and the will (*W2*, 207). For example, the will is a comparatively primitive part of us, and not sophisticated enough to react to imaginary ideas in a different way from genuine beliefs:

> If . . . we are alone, and think over our personal affairs, and then vividly picture to ourselves, say, the menace of an actually present danger, and the possibility of an unfortunate outcome, anxiety at once compresses the heart, and the blood ceases to flow. But if the intellect then passes to the possibility of the opposite outcome, and allows the imagination to picture the happiness long hoped-for as thereby attained, all the pulses at once quicken with joy, and the heart feels as light as a feather, until the intellect wakes up from its dream . . . We see that the intellect strikes up the tune, and the will must dance to it; in fact, the intellect causes it to play the part of a child whom its nurse at her pleasure puts into the most different moods by chatter and tales alternating between pleasant and melancholy things. (*W2*, 207–8)

On the other hand, our ordinary experience of the world is suffused with the positive or negative significance that comes from the will:

> In the immediate perception of the world and of life, we consider things as a rule merely in their relations . . . we regard houses, ships, machines, and the like with the idea of their purpose and their suitability therefor . . . Let us picture to ourselves how much every emotion or passion obscures and falsifies knowledge, in fact how every inclination or disinclination twists, colours, and distorts not merely the judgement, but even the original perception of things. Let us recall how, when we are delighted by a successful outcome, the whole world at once assumes a bright colour and a smiling aspect, and on the other hand looks dark and

gloomy when care and sorrow weigh on us. Let us then see how even an inanimate thing, which is yet to become the instrument for some event we abhor, appears to have a hideous physiognomy; for example the scaffold, the fortress to which we are taken, the surgeon's case of instruments, the travelling coach of loved ones, and so on. (*W2*, 372–3)

We tend not to use the intellect in a 'pure' fashion. The way we confront the world of objects in experience and thought is driven by the will – further evidence for Schopenhauer that the will is primary in us. He has many more examples of the bias the will exerts:

Our *advantage*, of whatever kind it may be, exercises a similar secret power over our judgement; what is in agreement with it at once seems to us fair, just, and reasonable ... A hypothesis, conceived and formed, makes us lynx-eyed for everything that confirms it, and blind to everything that contradicts it. What is opposed to our party, our plan, our wish, or our hope often cannot possibly be grasped and comprehended by us, whereas it is clear to the eyes of everyone else. (*W2*, 217–18)

Anybody wishing to describe the mind as a centre of pure perception and reasoning would have to overcome the considerable evidence Schopenhauer amasses (from anecdote, general observation, and introspection) for the contrary view, that our experience is largely governed by what fits our own aims, instincts, and emotional needs.

Where Schopenhauer shows uncommon insight is in his theory of the unconscious, one of the more important and influential aspects of his theory of the will. Since the will is something that operates independently of our conscious representation of reality, it can be credited with desires, aims, and feelings which are not consciously entertained by the thinking subject, but which nevertheless control his or her behaviour. One example (which he says is 'trifling and ridiculous', but nevertheless 'striking') is that when adding up our finances 'we make mistakes more frequently to our advantage than to our disadvantage, and this indeed without the least intention of dishonesty, but merely through the unconscious tendency to diminish our *debit* and increase our *credit*' (W2, 218). But this is merely a small instance of a widespread principle. Schopenhauer says that the intellect is often excluded from 'secret decisions of its own will'. I do not consciously decide what I wish to happen in a particular situation, but at a certain outcome I feel 'a jubilant, irresistible gladness, diffused over my whole being . . . to my own astonishment . . . [O]nly now does my intellect learn how firmly my will had already laid hold of the plan' (W2, 209).

The will is here a part of the individual's mind which adopts attitudes and guides overt behaviour despite remaining out of sight of the conscious intellect. Schopenhauer even recognizes a process similar to Freud's much later idea of repression:

> this will . . . makes its supremacy felt in the last resort. This it does by prohibiting the intellect from having certain representations, by absolutely preventing certain trains of thought from arising, because it knows, or in other words experiences from the self-same intellect, that they would arouse in it any one of the emotions previously described. It then curbs and restrains the intellect, and forces it to turn to other things . . . We often do not know what we desire or fear. For years we can have a desire without admitting it to ourselves or even letting it come to clear consciousness, because the intellect is not to know anything about it, since the good opinion we have of ourselves would inevitably suffer thereby. But if the wish is fulfilled, we get to know from our joy, not without a feeling of shame, that this is what we desired. (W2, 208–10)

In another interesting passage, Schopenhauer sees this mechanism as responsible for some forms of madness:

Every new adverse event must be assimilated by the intellect . . . but this operation itself is often very painful, and in most cases takes place only slowly and with reluctance. But soundness of mind can continue only in so far as this operation has been correctly carried out each time. On the other hand, if, in a particular case, the resistance and opposition of the will to the assimilation of some knowledge reaches such a degree that . . . certain events or circumstances are wholly suppressed for the intellect, because the will cannot bear the sight of them; and then, if the resultant gaps are arbitrarily filled up for the sake of the necessary connection; we then have madness. (W2, 400)

Sexuality and gender

Schopenhauer exaggerates in saying that all previous philosophers have 'ignored' sexual love ('I have no predecessors' [W2, 533]), and his dismissal of Plato's contribution in particular is unwarranted (W2, 532). Nevertheless, in talking so bluntly about sexuality, and in making it such a cornerstone of his philosophy, he is again unusually forward-looking for his day. Sex is ever-present in our minds, according to Schopenhauer, 'the public secret which must never be distinctly mentioned anywhere, but is always and everywhere understood to be the main thing' (W2, 571). 'It is the ultimate goal of almost all human effort; it has an unfavourable influence on the most important affairs, interrupts every hour the most serious occupations' (W2, 533). None of this is surprising on Schopenhauer's theory. The impulse to sexual intercourse is at the very core of our being, as an instinct which is the most direct and powerful manifestation of will to life in our bodies: 'the genitals', he is fond of telling us, 'are the focus of the will'.

Schopenhauer explains instinct as 'an action as if in accordance with the conception of an end or purpose, and yet entirely without such a conception' (W2, 540). Sexual behaviour and anatomy are directed at reproduction in a purpose-like manner. Reproduction may at times also be a conscious purpose, of course, but to the extent that his or her behaviour manifests instinct, the individual's conscious purposes are irrelevant. According to Schopenhauer, the procreative 'purpose' which sexual activity and its elaborate, all-pervading surroundings are directed towards, is actually a 'purpose' of the human species, a built-in drive to generate itself over again, for which the individual acts as a mere vehicle. The seriousness with which individuals pursue sexual goals reflects the magnitude of this underlying species-purpose.

Thus Schopenhauer sees the individual's sexual behaviour as at the beck and call of an impersonal force. His most striking way of putting this is to say that it is the will to life of the as yet unconceived offspring which draws a male and female partner together. Their view that they are acting wholly in their own interests out of individual desires towards another individual is a 'delusion' (*W2*, 538), and this delusion itself is a means by which 'nature can attain her end'. The 'longing of love' celebrated in poetry of all ages is on this account truly something external to the lover, and hence so powerful that the individual can scarcely contain it:

> this longing that closely associates the notion of an endless bliss with the possession of a definite woman, and an unutterable pain with the thought that this possession is not attainable; this longing and this pain of love cannot draw their material from the needs of an ephemeral individual. On the contrary, they are the sighs of the spirit of the species . . . The species alone has infinite life, and is therefore capable of infinite desire, infinite satisfaction, and infinite sufferings. But these are here imprisoned in the narrow breast of a mortal; no wonder, therefore, when such a breast seems ready to burst, and can find no expression for the infinite rapture or infinite pain with which it is filled. (*W2*, 551)

Schopenhauer also believes that once the ends of the species are fulfilled between lovers, their rapture and their delusion must eventually ebb away:

Forsaken by [the spirit of the species], the individual falls back into his original narrowness and neediness, and sees with surprise that, after so high, heroic, and infinite an effort, nothing has resulted for his pleasure but what is afforded by any sexual satisfaction. Contrary to expectation, he finds himself no happier than before; he notices that he has been the dupe of the will of the species. (W2, 557)

Of course, individuals will continue to feel sexual desire as a desire of their own directed towards a particular person, and will be conscious of the person's physical and mental attributes. Schopenhauer gives us a detailed list of the qualities that men supposedly look for in women (right age, health, proportion of skeleton, fullness of flesh, beauty of the face – in that order) and that women supposedly look for in men (right age, strength, courage). Looking away from such details, however, all the features of attraction are to be explained in the same way: they result from unconscious principles of selection through which the will of the species works to ensure the character of its next generation. Where the intention of intercourse is expressly not to generate offspring, Schopenhauer is nevertheless determined to explain subjective attraction in terms of life-generating instincts. Even the case of homosexuality does not deter him: such a widespread practice must 'arise in some way from human nature itself', he thinks, though his explanation for it is somewhat desperate. Very young and very old males, he supposes, have deficient semen, and are following an instinct to discharge it in non-procreative fashion, thus still subserving the 'will of the species' for the best possible offspring.

Some may find surprising another of Schopenhauer's convictions: that it is the intellect which we inherit from our mothers, and the will from our fathers. Not many philosophers have thought of the intellect as a female characteristic, and the capacity for emotions as male. Schopenhauer is convinced that there is empirical evidence for his claim, but he also gives another argument in which he shows his true colours. The will is 'the true inner being, the kernel, the radical element', while the intellect is 'the secondary, the adventitious, the accident of that substance' (W2, 517). So, the argument continues, we should expect the more powerful, procreative sex to impart the will to its offspring, while the mother, the 'merely conceiving principle', is responsible for the merely secondary intellect. The agenda here is to make sure that the female comes out as superficial and secondary, the male as substantial, radical, and primary. What is inherited from the father is the 'moral nature', the 'character', the 'heart'. The view that the intellect is female in origin thus results from a cross-fertilization between Schopenhauer's doctrine of the metaphysical primacy of the will and his fairly conventional prejudice that the female must be secondary to the male.

Schopenhauer's disparaging view of women, concentrated to most corrosive effect in the short essay 'On Women' (P2, 614–26), has earned him some notoriety. To what extent it should single him out from any of his contemporaries and predecessors is debatable. On the one hand, he is perhaps especially worthy of note because of his attempt to imbue gender differences with such metaphysical significance, and because he gives such prominence to sexuality in human life. On the other hand, it may be thought that his actual views are fairly commonplace for his time. What is not in question is the vehemence of his rhetoric on the topic:

> Only the male intellect, clouded by the sexual impulse, could call the undersized, narrow-shouldered, broad-hipped, and short-legged sex the fair sex; for in this impulse is to be found its whole beauty. (P2, 619)

> Throughout their lives women remain children, always see only what is nearest to them, cling to the present, take the appearance of things for reality, and prefer trivialities to the most important affairs. Thus it is the faculty of reason by virtue whereof man does not, like the animals, live merely in the present . . . In consequence of her weaker faculty of reason, woman shares less in the advantages and disadvantages that this entails. (P2, 615–16)

63

There are a few compensating virtues. Schopenhauer allots to women the greater share of humane loving-kindness, which for him is of supreme moral worth; he also thinks they are more down-to-earth and practical than men (the intellect at work again); but he is convinced that they cannot reason very well, and have shallow characters. Their interests are 'love, conquests, dress, cosmetics, dancing'; they regard everything as a means to winning a man; dissimulation is inborn to them 'just as nature has armed the lion with claws and teeth, the elephant and boar with tusks, the bull with horns, and the cuttle-fish with ink that blackens water' (*P2*, 617). Women may be talented, but artistic geniuses can, apparently, only be male: 'generally speaking, women are and remain the most downright and incurable Philistines' (*P2*, 620-1). Occasionally, one glimpses a portrait of the novelist, socialite, and mother Johanna Schopenhauer:

the original maternal love is purely *instinctive* and therefore ceases with the physical helplessness of the children. In its place, there should then appear one based on habit and reasoning; but often it fails to appear, especially when the mother has not loved the father ... Property acquired by the long and constant hard work of men subsequently passes into the hands of women who in their folly get through it or otherwise squander it in a short time ... The vanity of women ... is bad because it is centred entirely on material things ... and hence society is so very much their element. (*P2*, 625-6)

Conventional male sentiment mixed with personal bitterness – the result is scarcely edifying. But no account of Schopenhauer's philosophy ought to suppress these ideas, which were clearly important to him.

Character

We have seen that in Schopenhauer's view the will is the primary element within us, the intellect only secondary and 'adventitious'. In this, the will often has the role of an impersonal force which is greater than the individual, attaching to the species or to the world as a whole, and expressing itself in each individual equally. However, Schopenhauer also believes that each person has a distinct character. And here too the intellect is secondary. It is not intellectual abilities and traits, or continuity of consciousness, that marks out the true core of one's separate identity as an individual.

> The older we become, the more does everything pass us by without leaving a trace. Great age, illness, injury to the brain, madness, can deprive a man entirely of memory, but the identity of his person has not in this way been lost. That rests on the identical *will* and on its unalterable character; it is also just this that makes the expression of the glance unalterable. . . . Our true self . . . really knows nothing but willing and not-willing, being contented and not contented, with all the modifications of the thing called feelings, emotions, and passions. (*W2*, 239)

Each human being's character is unique for Schopenhauer, though since we all belong to the same species, the differences may sometimes be very slight. Individual character comes into its own in explaining and predicting actions. An action follows on from motives, but only in combination with the character of the agent. The same set of objective circumstances, perceived and comprehended in the same way by different people, may lead them to act in quite different ways. Offer a large bribe and some will take it, some will politely decline, and others will turn you over to the authorities. The motive, in Schopenhauer's sense (that is, the external state of affairs as apprehended by the intellect) can be the same in all three cases, and the intellect itself can, if you like, be working in exactly the same way. But the character is what differs. If we knew each person's character thoroughly, and all the motives they were exposed to, we could predict all their actions without any remainder. In another of Schopenhauer's beloved Latin tags, *operari sequitur esse*, 'acting follows from being': what we *are* partly determines how we act. The principle is no different from that by which we predict the varied behaviour of different natural substances under the same influence: 'the effect of the same motive on different people is quite different; as the sunlight gives to wax white colour and to chloric silver black, so the heat makes wax soft, but clay hard' (*F*, 50). This doctrine of character has consequences for freedom, responsibility, and morality, as we shall discover later.

Schopenhauer sees the character as a person's 'being', something distinct from the collection of all the person's actions put together. The actions follow from the being, each of them bearing the stamp of the person to whom they belong. This may make the character sound mysterious, but Schopenhauer assures us that we only ever learn about it, in other people or even in ourselves, from its empirical manifestations – just the way we learn about the character of wax or chloric silver, in fact. We observe many actions, and come to know someone's degree of honesty, courage, or compassion over the course of time. Similarly with ourselves: until we see how we fare in action, we may be quite wrong about the qualities of character which we possess. So Schopenhauer says that character is *empirical*. It is not identical with the series of actions I carry out, yet is discovered only from observation of those actions.

Schopenhauer maintains that each person's character is both constant and inborn. We can neither choose nor change what we are. We can be educated to understand the world and ourselves better, giving us better, more refined motives on which to act, but the self that these motives prompt into action really has not altered: 'Under the changeable shell of his years, his relationships, and even his store of knowledge and opinions, there hides, like a crab under its shell, the identical and real man, quite unchangeable and always the same' (*F*, 51). Schopenhauer thinks that many of our ordinary attitudes bear out this claim: we assume not just identity of the person, but constancy in the moral character as well. When we have gone on trusting someone to behave in a certain way, and have eventually been disappointed, 'we never say: "His character has changed", but "I was mistaken about him"' (*F*, 52). For example, we say, on this view, not that someone used to be honest and courageous, but is now deceitful and cowardly; rather that the extent of their deceitfulness and cowardice was not fully apparent until now. As further evidence for constancy of character Schopenhauer cites the fact that we recognize others as the same after many years from the manner in which they act, and that we feel responsibility and shame for things we ourselves did forty years before.

With the claim that character is inborn we again find that human beings are to be treated very much on a par with other parts of nature. You would not try to produce apricots from an oak tree, says Schopenhauer. Human beings clearly have inborn species-characteristics. Why are people so loath to accept that there is inborn courage, honesty, or wickedness at the level of the individual? Schopenhauer's evidence, such as it is, leads him to think that the human individual at birth cannot be a mere blank slate which awaits experience before it forms any character at all. Before we can have knowledge or perceive the world very well, we are creatures of will, reacting with positive or negative feelings to what impinges on us. Even at this stage, there is a basic core to the person which is not moulded by what he or she has intellectually apprehended of the world.

Schopenhauer also has the notion of *acquired character*. Especially when we are young, we may not correctly understand what our character is. We do not know what we really like, or want, or can succeed at. Acquired character is a better self-understanding, which one comes to have by gaining an insight into one's true constant character – an idea in some ways reminiscent of Nietzsche's later notion of 'becoming who you are'. This enlightened idea is, however, at odds with the rest of Schopenhauer's account. For it seems that before I have attained the acquired character, I may embark on ventures that go against my real nature – which ought to be impossible if my inborn, unchanging character determines all my actions.

Sometimes, however, Schopenhauer says things about the character which are even more puzzling.

> however old we become, we yet feel within ourselves that we are absolutely the same as we were when we were young . . . This thing which is unaltered and always remains absolutely the same, which does not grow old with us, is just the kernel of our inner nature, and that does not lie in time . . . [W]e are accustomed to regard the subject of knowing, the knowing I, as our real self . . . This, however, is the mere function of the brain, and is not our real self. Our true self . . . it is which produces that other thing, which does not sleep with it when it sleeps, which also remains unimpaired when that other thing becomes extinct in death . . . The *character itself* . . . is still exactly the same now as then. The will itself, alone and by itself, endures; for it alone is unchangeable, indestructible, does not grow old, is not physical but metaphysical, does not belong to the phenomenal appearance, but to the thing in itself that appears. (*W*2, 238–9)

Here it is unclear what kind of thing the character is. On the one hand it is unique and attaches to oneself as an individual. On the other hand it is 'not in time', it is 'not physical but metaphysical', and even 'remains unimpaired' when the individual dies and his or her subjective consciousness disappears. The problem, bluntly, is this: is my 'real self', or 'the kernel of my inner nature', something that attaches to the finite individual that I am, or is it the thing in itself, beyond space, time, and individuation altogether? If the former, it is neither outside of time nor unaffected by my own death. If the latter, it does not serve to explain my personal identity at all. Schopenhauer seems to stumble into a quite elementary difficulty. But in a way his confusion has a more profound point behind it. For he wants to claim in the end that our individuality, seemingly so fundamental to us, is not only a source of torment, but some kind of illusion: 'at bottom every individuality is really only a special error, a false step, something that it would be better should not be' (*W*2, 491–2). The Third and Fourth Books of *The World as Will and*

Representation – its great second half to which we now turn – explore the possibilities of escaping from individuality, and from the will which lies at our core.

Chapter 6
Art and ideas

Aesthetic experience

Aesthetic experience deliberately reverses the trend of Schopenhauer's book, for in it the will of the subject is suspended. As long as we exercise the will, or are governed by it, we shall be forced to consider a thing in a great mesh of relations to other things and to ourselves: Do we want it? Can we use it? Is it better than something else? What made it the way it is? What will it make happen? Just as our intellects are organs developed to subserve the will, so all the usual connections which we employ in order to understand objects are will-governed: we perceive in order to manipulate, in order to live. Only if we cease to will at all can the object stand out in our consciousness stripped of the relations of time, place, cause, and effect.

Schopenhauer belongs to a tradition which equates aesthetic experience with a 'disinterested' attitude towards its object, and is often cited as one of the chief proponents of such a view. The idea is that to experience something aesthetically, one must suspend or disengage all one's desires towards it, attending not to any consideration of what ends, needs, or interests it may fulfil, but only to the way it presents itself in perception. In Schopenhauer's case, aesthetic experience must always be an extraordinary episode in any human being's life, since he has argued that the will is our essence, and that our 'ordinary way of considering things' is permeated by will:

> so long as our consciousness is filled by our will, so long as we are given up to the throng of desires with its constant hopes and fears, so long as we are the subject of willing, we never attain lasting happiness or peace. . . . Thus the subject of willing is constantly lying on the revolving wheel of Ixion, is always drawing water in the sieve of the Danaids, and is the eternally thirsting Tantalus.

> When, however, an external cause or inward disposition suddenly raises us out of the endless stream of willing, and snatches knowledge from the thraldom of the will, the attention is now no longer directed to the motives of willing, but comprehends things free from their relation to the will. Thus it considers things without interest, without subjectivity, purely objectively . . . Then all at once the peace, always sought but always escaping us on that first path of willing, comes to us of its own accord, and all is well with us . . . [F]or that moment we are delivered from the miserable pressure of the will. We celebrate the Sabbath of the penal servitude of willing; the wheel of Ixion stands still. (W1, 196)

After the brisk formality of the opening book on the world as representation, and the incipient gloom as we descend into the world as will, the Third Book of *The World as Will and Representation* has a character of brightness and joy, which testifies to the importance of the aesthetic for its author.

Schopenhauer states the central problem of aesthetics in an acute way: 'how satisfaction with and pleasure in an object are possible without any reference thereto to our willing' (*P2*, 415). (His view of aesthetic enjoyment is similar in some respects to that put forward by Kant in his *Critique of Judgement*, though Schopenhauer makes little of this connection, and does not rate Kant's work on aesthetics as among his best.) In the usual run of events, pleasure or satisfaction arises from the

8. Schopenhauer: portrait by Julius Hamel, 1856

fulfilment of some desire or end. What we call happiness is usually felt on attaining one of our ends, or it may be the temporary absence of anything further to strive for. But these kinds of pleasure and happiness, since they depend on willing, also carry with them the permanent possibility of suffering. In the first place, all willing 'springs from lack, from deficiency, and thus from suffering' (W1, 196). Secondly, when any particular desire is stilled, the subject of willing soon experiences another deficiency. Thus to be driven by the will is to oscillate between suffering and satisfaction, and Schopenhauer is convinced that the suffering lasts longer, the satisfaction being only a temporary return to neutral before another lack is felt.

The problem for aesthetics is how there can be any kind of pleasure other than that which is contained in this oscillation. If pleasure is defined as the fulfilment of a lack or the satisfaction of a desire, then a totally will-less state of contemplation ought to be one in which one cannot experience pleasure at all. Clearly, the positive gain of being in such a state would be the loss of the possibility of suffering, and Schopenhauer makes a great deal of this point. But how could a will-less state leave room for real pleasure? Sometimes Schopenhauer writes as if it could not, as if aesthetic contemplation were a state purely of knowledge, a dispassionate registering of objective reality – 'we have stepped into another world, so to speak, where everything that moves our will, and thus violently agitates us, no longer exists. . . . Happiness and unhappiness have vanished' (W1, 197). Yet he is also prepared to describe aesthetic experience in terms such as 'peace' and 'blessedness', and as a special kind of pleasure or enjoyment. He even states that when 'all possibility of suffering is abolished . . . the state of pure objectivity of perception becomes one that makes us feel positively happy' (W2, 368). These different claims can be reconciled by saying that the usual kind of happiness (and unhappiness) depends on willing, while the aesthetic kind depends on the cessation of willing.

This might be thought sufficient to give aesthetic experience the value which Schopenhauer wishes to assign it. However, his version of the 'aesthetic attitude' theory is unusual in linking the state of will-less contemplation with the achievement of the most objective kind of knowledge. For him, an experience undergone in the absence of subjective desires and aims will be one which distorts the world as little as possible, so he can maintain that aesthetic experience is valuable not only for the calming effect of escaping from one's own will, but because it uniquely displays things as they eternally are. Aesthetic experience, in other words, has high cognitive value, not merely the enriching or therapeutic value of entering into a certain psychological state.

Objectivity and genius

The subject ordinarily experiences material objects that occupy space and time, their causal connections to one another, and bodily acts of will following upon motives. But Schopenhauer believes that we can in exceptional moments gain access to a timeless reality that is not carved up into individuals. Beyond the realm of individual things and events lies the Idea, to which 'neither plurality nor change' belongs: 'While the individuals in which it expresses itself are innumerable and are incessantly coming into existence and passing away, it remains unchanged as one and the same, and the principle of sufficient reason has no meaning for it' (W1, 169).

Schopenhauer begins his Third Book with a disquisition on Platonic Ideas and their relation to the thing in itself. His claim will be that artists, and all engaged in aesthetic experience, discern, however fleetingly, the timeless reality of Ideas. Hence he owes us an attempt to set the metaphysical record straight first: what are these Ideas? He calls them 'the most adequate objectivity' of the thing in itself. This sounds obscure but is in fact quite a simple notion. The thing in itself cannot be known; but a knowable object which presented reality to the subject with the least possible degree of subjective distortion would be the 'adequate objectivity' of the thing in itself. Thus Schopenhauer explains:

> the Platonic Idea is necessarily object, something known, a representation, and precisely, but only, in this respect is it different from the thing in itself. It has laid aside merely the subordinate forms of the phenomenon, all of which we include under the principle of sufficient reason; or rather it has not yet entered into them. But it has retained the first and most universal form, namely that of the representation in general, that of being object for a subject. . . . Therefore, it alone is the most *adequate objectivity* possible of the will or of the thing in itself; indeed it is even the whole thing in itself, only under the form of the representation. Here lies the ground of the great agreement between Plato and Kant, although in strict accuracy that of which they both speak is not the same. (W1, 175)

Some strain is evident in the way that the Idea seems forced to serve as both thing in itself and representation, when these two categories were supposedly mutually exclusive at the outset. Also, although he recognizes that the equation of Kant and Plato would be wrong 'in strict accuracy', he is still prepared to make the extremely dubious statement that 'the inner meaning of both doctrines is wholly the same' (*W1*, 172). Some commentators have regarded the Ideas as an awkward, hasty afterthought. This is not wholly a fair assessment, however, as the Ideas were one of the earliest parts of the system to fall into place, and figured in the account of the will's objectification in nature in the Second Book. What we should hold on to is the notion that nature contains not only a multiplicity of individual things and events, but unchanging single kinds to which they belong. There are not only horses, but the species *horse*, not only pools and fountains but the repeatable molecular structure H_2O, not only many bodies falling to the ground at different times and places, but a ubiquitous gravitational force. Schopenhauer thinks of such kinds as timeless Ideas, and our apprehension of them as the most objective knowledge of the world we can ever attain. Schopenhauer follows Plato in claiming that Ideas exist in reality, independently of the subject. They are not concepts. Concepts are the mental constructs we make in order to grasp reality in general terms; but Ideas are parts of nature awaiting discovery. For Schopenhauer, they are not even discovered by conceptual thinking, but by perception and imagination.

What would consciousness of Ideas themselves be like? Schopenhauer has a dramatic answer. Once we abandon the guidance of the principle of sufficient reason,

> we no longer consider the where, the when, the why, and the whither of things, but simply and solely the *what*. ... [We] let our whole consciousness be filled by the calm contemplation of the natural object actually present, whether it be a landscape, a tree, a rock, a crag, a building, or anything else . . . and continue to exist only as pure subject, as clear mirror of the object, so that it is as though the object alone

existed without anyone to perceive it, and thus we are no longer able to separate the perceiver from the perception. . . . What is thus known is no longer the individual thing as such, but the *Idea* . . . at the same time, the person who is involved in this perception is no longer an individual, for in such perception the individual has lost himself; he is *pure* will-less, painless, timeless *subject of knowledge*. (*W1*, 178–9)

'At one stroke', Schopenhauer continues, the particular thing 'becomes the Idea of its species', and the perceiving individual 'becomes the *pure subject* of *knowing*' (*W1*, 179). What Schopenhauer must mean is that I see the particular as embodying a universal Idea, and momentarily lose consciousness of myself as an individual. His claim is that one cannot know Ideas if one retains an awareness of oneself as an individual separate from the object contemplated ('we apprehend the world purely objectively, only when we no longer know that we belong to it' [*W2*, 368]) – and conversely that one cannot fail to be knowing an Idea, once one's contemplation turns one into this 'pure mirror' of reality.

Although Schopenhauer clearly thinks that natural beauty often gives rise to aesthetic experience (witness the examples of tree, rock, and crag), it is to art that he gives most attention. He is fairly orthodox for his day in believing that the production of art requires something called genius, which must be distinguished from mere talent. But he does give his own account of what genius is. It consists, he writes, 'in the knowing faculty having received a considerably more powerful development than is required by the *service of the will*' (*W2*, 377). The person of genius has two-thirds intellect and one-third will, the 'normal person' is the other way round. It is not that the genius is lacking in will – such people usually have strong emotions, for example – but rather that their intellect is capable of detaching itself from the will to a much greater extent, and has the power to function autonomously:

the *gift of genius* is nothing but the most complete *objectivity* . . . the capacity to remain in a state of pure perception, to lose oneself in perception, to remove from the service of the will the knowledge which originally existed only for this service. In other words, genius is the ability to leave entirely out of sight our own interest, our willing, and our aims, and consequently to discard entirely our own personality for a time, in order to remain *pure knowing subject*, the clear eye of the world; and this not merely for moments, but with the necessary continuity and conscious thought to enable us to repeat by deliberate art what has been apprehended. (*W1*, 185-6)

The genius stands for something impersonal, which Schopenhauer hints at with the metaphor of 'the clear eye of the world'. The genius is not only an individual, but 'at the same time a pure intellect that as such belongs to the whole of mankind' (*W2*, 390). Abandoning the will that manifests itself in this particular individual, and letting the intellect soar free of it, the genius has an uncommon ability 'to see the universal in the particular' (*W2*, 379). It is important that this is a capacity for heightened *perception*. A great painter or sculptor *sees* with more intensity and more detail, and has greater ability to retain and reproduce what is seen. But perceiving merely what is present to hand is not enough: '*imagination* is needed, in order to complete, arrange, amplify, fix, retain, and repeat at pleasure all the significant pictures of life' (*W2*, 379). Thus genius, in whichever art form, may go one better than actual experience: a great work of art may reflect reality all the better when the picture it conveys is a heightened one, having more clarity and definition than is ever contained in ordinary experience itself.

The true province of genius is imaginative perception, and not conceptual thinking. Art which is structured around some proposition, or worked out on a wholly rational plan, is dead and uninteresting by comparison. One example is where pictorial art turns to a symbolic form of allegory, and can be grasped only by deciphering images according to a code, something alien to art as such, in Schopenhauer's view (*W1*, 239). Another is when 'imitators' or 'mannerists' set themselves to produce according to a formula which they note to have been successful in some other work. The result is offensive: prior deliberation can always be discerned, and the constituent elements they have minced together can always be 'picked out and separated from the mixture'. The concept, 'useful as it is in life, serviceable, necessary, and productive as it is in science, is eternally barren and unproductive in art' (*W1*, 235).

Geniuses are rare because they are in a sense unnatural. In the great majority of people, the workings of the intellect are subordinate to the attainment of individual ends, as Schopenhauer's theory would predict. The intellect is an instrument of the will, and is not 'designed' for purposeless imaginative work which grasps and relays eternal Ideas. By the same token, people possessed of genius are commonly viewed as oddities. With its heightened imagination and tendency to distract from the immediate connections of things, genius has some resemblance to madness. Geniuses do not accommodate to the expectations of their own time and place, unlike people of mere talent, who are admired for the ability to produce what is wanted when it is wanted (*W2*, 390). The genius is also prone to impracticality, because of the degree to which his intellect works independently of the end-seeking will. (I say 'his', because Schopenhauer does not recognize female genius, even though the intellect is supposedly a female inheritance. The difference is presumably supposed to be that women's perception always remains superficial and never rises to 'the universal'.)

The arts and their value

Schopenhauer commands respect among historians of aesthetics for his deep and varied knowledge of the arts. While he has a single theory of aesthetic appreciation as the will-less contemplation of Ideas, he appreciates many different art forms, from architecture through painting of different genres, to poetry and drama, and eventually to music, which he sets apart from the rest. His aesthetics is not an inflexible metaphysical monolith: its core is fleshed out with elegance and sensitivity.

Before discussing the various arts, Schopenhauer makes a substantial qualification to his theory. He has claimed that whenever we have an aesthetic experience there occurs both a subjective cessation of willing and an objective insight into the realm of Ideas. However, he now admits that the value of a particular object of aesthetic experience can reside in one or other of these factors almost to the exclusion of the other:

> with aesthetic contemplation (in real life or through the medium of art) of natural beauty in the inorganic and vegetable kingdoms and of the works of architecture, the enjoyment of pure, will-less knowing will predominate, because the Ideas here apprehended are only low grades of the will's objectivity, and therefore are not phenomena of deep significance and suggestive content. On the other hand, if animals and human beings are the object of aesthetic contemplation or presentation, the enjoyment will consist rather in the objective apprehension of these Ideas. (W1, 212)

In other words, the cognitive import of aesthetic experience may often be quite low. This may invite the thought that the single unifying element in his aesthetics is really the notion of pleasurable will-free contemplation, or even that his aesthetics is not unified. However, he deserves credit for realizing that the arts are regarded both as a release from the pressures of living, and as an intense form of knowledge.

The Ideas form a hierarchy of higher and lower grades of the will's objectification. The lowest are the all-pervading natural forces, the highest the Idea of humanity. Architecture is the art form that deals with the lowest Ideas concerning the behaviour of solid matter: gravity, cohesion, rigidity, and hardness (W1, 214). Buildings must also be of practical use, so that their potential to be pure art is, or should be, restricted. But the real core of architecture as an art is the conflict between gravity and rigidity. All the parts of a fine building should be relevant to making this conflict manifest to the observer, and should appear necessary rather than arbitrary: merely decorative elements belong to sculpture, and not to architecture as such. Also, it matters what materials a building is made from. An edifice which turned out to be of wood or pumice-stone would be a kind of sham, because materials less substantial than stone are not suited to bring out the Ideas of gravity and rigidity. We must be able to grasp in our perception the striving of the blocks towards the earth, and the counter-striving of the rigid elements which prevent them from falling. All else is irrelevant – mere beauty of shape is not a peculiarly architectural feature. The only other aspect to architecture that Schopenhauer acknowledges is light. The illumination of a building serves to reveal its fundamental structure more clearly, while that structure, by intercepting and reflecting light, 'unfolds [light's] nature and qualities in the purest and clearest way, to the great delight of the beholder' (*W1*, 216). Similar to architecture is 'the artistic arrangement of water' (*W1*, 217), which is less developed as an art simply because it is less useful than the making of buildings. The construction of fountains, waterfalls, and lakes does for the Ideas of fluidity, mobility, and transparency what architecture does for those of rigidity and cohesion.

Horticulture and landscaping provide a parallel in the realm of plants, although here Schopenhauer reckons that it is predominantly nature rather than art that does the work. Only in depictions of vegetation in painting does art come into its own. Our aesthetic enjoyment of a landscape painting whose subject is entirely vegetative or inanimate is one where 'the subjective side of aesthetic pleasure is predominant', residing in pure, will-less knowing, rather than in apprehending Ideas (*W1*, 218). But painting and sculpture become more concerned with the objective depiction of Ideas when they take animals and finally human beings as their subjects. Schopenhauer sees no important difference between confronting a person or animal face to face, and looking at an artistic representation – except that the abilities of a genius allow art to provide us with exemplars of greater beauty than nature actually provides: the genius 'impresses on the hard marble the beauty of form which nature failed to achieve in a thousand attempts, and he places it before her, exclaiming as it were, "This is what you desired to say!"' (*W1*, 222).

With depicted animals, as with animals themselves, the most beautiful individual is the one most characteristic of the species (*W1*, 220) – the lion, for example, in which we are best able to see the universal Idea of *the lion* embodied. Here, what we enjoy is less the calm of will-less contemplation, more our getting to know the animal which we see in the painting or sculpture: 'we are occupied with the restlessness and impetuosity of the depicted will' (*W1*, 219). With human beings, it is also true that the beautiful individual is the one most characteristic of the species. But there are also considerations of individual character and expression: a portrait ought to bring out the universal Idea of humanity, but of course must render the particular character of the sitter. Is this not an objection to Schopenhauer's theory that the point of art is always to express Ideas? May the strength of a work of art not lie in its conveying something particular and even arbitrary? Schopenhauer attempts to preserve the unity of his theory by maintaining that 'each person exhibits to a certain extent an Idea that is wholly characteristic of him' (*W1*, 224). But if apprehending an Idea is not always apprehending something timeless, universal, and potentially common to many individuals, it surely becomes less clear what sense we may attach to the notion.

Many paintings depict scenes from history, or from some particular legend or biblical story. But again, Schopenhauer urges that what makes them artistically significant is the extent to which they express something universal about mankind. Particular historical circumstances are irrelevant: 'it is all the same as regards inward significance whether ministers dispute about countries and nations over a map, or boors in a beer-house choose to wrangle over cards and dice' (*W1*, 231). Schopenhauer is fond of contrasting the arts with history. He takes a high-handed line, and often uses the opportunity to disagree with the Hegelian conception of history. In his view, the essential kernel of human beings is always the same, not liable to local variation or change over time. Thus he makes the startling pronouncement that 'The chapters of the history of nations are at bottom different only through the names and dates; the really essential content is everywhere the same' (*W2*, 442). History, he maintains, co-ordinates merely facts about the changing surface of humanity, and can never get beyond this. The contrasting form of discourse is poetry: 'paradoxical as it may sound, far more real, genuine, inner truth is to be attributed to poetry than to history' (*W1*, 245). 'Genuine, inner truth' is supposedly truth about what does not change, that is, the Idea of humanity.

Poetry emerges as the art form which is able to express the Idea of absolutely anything in the world, but which reigns supreme in portraying the diverse characters and actions of mankind. Again Schopenhauer distinguishes carefully between concepts, which are abstract representations formed by the subject, and Ideas, which can be accessed in direct experience and are part of the fabric of nature itself. The task for the poet is to use the conceptual means which poetry has in common with other linguistic practices, towards the distinctive end of revealing an Idea to the mind of the reader. It is this that marks poetry out as an artistic use of language, and as the province of genius – for the writer cannot make an Idea perspicuous to the reader unless he or she first has sufficient objectivity to perceive it. Poetry can be called 'the art of bringing into play the power of imagination through words' (*W2*, 424). It differs from the visual arts not only in using language, but in the degree of work that must be done by the imagination of the recipient. Schopenhauer says much that is of interest about the different genres and styles of poetry: lyric, epic, and tragic, romantic and classical (which he prefers). Sometimes the poet finds the material, the Idea of humanity in him- or herself, the result of which is lyric poetry. At the other end of the spectrum lies drama, in which the writer depicts humanity from an objective point of view.

Schopenhauer gives particular attention to tragedy, as the 'summit of poetic art' (*W1*, 252). While he is not alone in considering tragedy a supreme art form, it has especial importance for him because it is uniquely able to portray human life in what he regards as its true colours, containing the right degree of unfulfilled desire, conflict, and unmitigated suffering: 'It is the antagonism of the will with itself which is here most completely unfolded at the highest grade of its objectivity' (*W1*, 253). But seeing the Idea of humanity revealed in all its terrible truth is not the end of the matter. Schopenhauer requires that we understand also the ultimate human achievement (as he will later argue it to be) of resigning oneself, and turning against the will to life: 'we see in tragedy the noblest men, after a long conflict and suffering, finally renounce for ever all the pleasures of life and the aims till then pursued so keenly, or cheerfully and willingly give up life itself' (*W1*, 253).

Witnessing the depiction of suffering and resignation in tragedy, we learn by suffering in some measure ourselves. The best kind of tragedy, in Schopenhauer's view (which admittedly leaves out many famous instances of the genre) is where a catastrophe occurs in the course of a more or less ordinary life through no particularly grave fault of the protagonist. This kind of tragedy 'shows us those powers that destroy happiness and life, and in such a way that the path to them is at any moment open even to us. . . . Then, shuddering, we feel ourselves already in the midst of hell' (*W1*, 255). Is there room for pure aesthetic pleasure amid such terror – amid such perturbations of the will? Schopenhauer's answer invokes the Kantian conception of the sublime, in which the contemplation of something potentially destructive, viewed from the vantage point of present safety, brings a pleasurable sense of elevation. Schopenhauer gives this his own twist, however. What we rise to, above our shudderings at the depicted pain and misery of the tragedy, is, he claims, a sense of the serene abandonment of all willing which beckons from the very highest plateau that human life can reach. 'What gives to everything tragic . . . the characteristic tendency to the sublime, is the dawning of the knowledge that the world and life can afford us no true satisfaction, and are therefore not worth our attachment to them' (*W2*, 433–4).

Music

Schopenhauer's philosophical theory of music is set apart from his account of the other arts, and has enjoyed something of a life of its own in musical circles and in aesthetics. It remains one of the most striking theories of the power of music to express emotion, even if, like other attempts to explain this phenomenon, it is not ultimately convincing. Schopenhauer's view is that music is a 'copy of the will itself' (*W1*, 257). Whereas all the other art forms present us with Ideas which are the experienceable manifestation of the will, music bypasses these Ideas, and is 'as *immediate* an objectification and copy of the whole *will* as the world itself is'. The will expresses itself once as the whole world of particular phenomena and universal kinds into which they fall; it expresses itself over again as music. There are two parts to Schopenhauer's view. One attempts to explain the significance of music in terms of states of feeling and striving that we are familiar with in ourselves. The other draws a large-scale analogy between the range of phenomena in nature and the different elements of which music consists.

Here is Schopenhauer's idea about music and conscious strivings:

> The nature of man consists in the fact that his will strives, is satisfied, strives anew, and so on and on; in fact his happiness and well-being consist only in the transition from desire to satisfaction, and from this to a fresh desire . . . Thus, corresponding to this, the nature of melody is a constant digression and deviation from the keynote in a thousand

ways ... [M]elody expresses the many different forms of the will's
efforts, but also its satisfaction by ultimately finding again a harmonious
interval, and still more the keynote. (*W1*, 260)

Schopenhauer contends that the progression of musical notes through
time is immediately understood by the human mind as an analogy of
the progress of our own inner strivings. Here are some of the many
examples he gives:

as rapid transition from wish to satisfaction and from this to a new wish
are happiness and well-being, so rapid melodies without great deviations
are cheerful. Slow melodies that strike painful discords and wind back to
the keynote only through many bars, are sad, on the analogy of delayed
and hard-won satisfaction. ... The *adagio* speaks of the suffering
of a great and noble endeavour that disdains all trifling happiness.
(*W1*, 260–1)

The effect of the *suspension* also deserves to be considered here. It is a
dissonance delaying the final consonance that is with certainty awaited;
in this way the longing for it is strengthened, and its appearance affords
the greater satisfaction. This is clearly an analogue of the satisfaction of
the will which is enhanced through delay. (*W2*, 455–6)

Many have found these ideas reflected especially in the composition of
Wagner's *Tristan and Isolde*.

A popular prejudice is that music expresses the emotion of the
composer or performer. But this is decidedly not Schopenhauer's view.
Music, for him, has the peculiarity of expressing what might be called
impersonal emotions:

music does not express this or that particular and definite pleasure, this
or that affliction, pain, sorrow, horror, gaiety, merriment, or peace of
mind, but joy, pain, sorrow, horror, gaiety, merriment, peace of mind

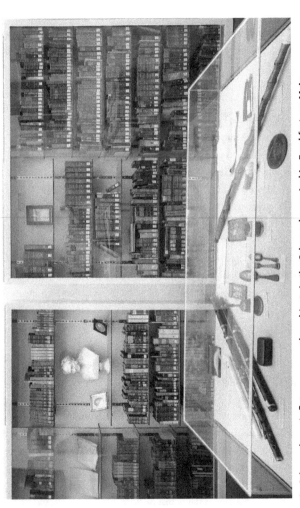

9. Schopenhauer's flutes among other objects in the Schopenhauer-Archiv, Frankfurt am Main

themselves, to a certain extent in the abstract, their essential nature, without any accessories, and so also without the motives for them. (*W1*, 261)

If a person experiences some particular joy or sorrow in life, usually some 'motive' or representation of the way things are gives rise to the emotion. Emotions tend to be about something. But Schopenhauer is proposing that in music we grasp directly and non-conceptually the essential shape, as it were, of feeling joy or sorrow without any content – without any representation of what the emotion is about. Listeners thus recognize the pure ebb and flow of the will, of striving and satisfaction, in which their own life consists, but without their own desires being engaged, without feeling emotions themselves, and so without any risk of pain. The account remains intriguing, though we may question whether it really captures the essential nature of the emotions, or explains just how the listener is supposed to apprehend them.

Schopenhauer's other central thought about music is that it parallels the world in the range of expressions of will which it achieves. The bass is like the lowest grade of the will's objectification, 'inorganic nature, the mass of the planet' (*W1*, 258). The melody on top is analogous to 'the highest grade of the will's objectification, the intellectual life and endeavour of man' (*W1*, 259). All the parts in between, with their intervals from one another, are the various manifestations of will throughout the inorganic world and the plant and animal kingdoms. Hence, music is not merely an expression of conscious human strivings, but a copy of the will in its great diversity, and hence a re-run of the whole phenomenal world. This idea, though fanciful, is a rather fine one. Whether or not Schopenhauer's views about music can be subscribed to literally, one can understand why musicians have often been drawn to him. No other philosopher has given music such a weighty role, and few have come nearer to the impossible achievement of evoking its pleasures in a purely verbal medium.

Chapter 7
Ethics: seeing the world aright

Against Kant's ethics

In Schopenhauer's view, the ethical sphere parallels the aesthetic in that prescriptive rules, and conceptual thought in general, are not the essential thing:

> Virtue is as little taught as is genius; indeed, the concept is just as unfruitful for it as it is for art, and in the case of both can be used only as an instrument. We should therefore be just as foolish to expect that our moral systems and ethics would create virtuous, noble, and holy men, as that our aesthetics would produce poets, painters, and musicians. (W1, 271)

This suggests that people will either have intuitive ethical insight or they will not; and we know that Schopenhauer thinks an individual's basic character cannot be altered. Moral rules, in that case, are useful only in channelling and curbing people's behaviour: you can train an egoistic person so that his or her behaviour has less disastrous consequences, but not make him or her into a good person. Since he takes this view, Schopenhauer's philosophical ethics will not itself be prescriptive. Nor will it attempt to debate whether moral laws are universally binding, or consider what reason one has to obey them, or indeed give any theory of 'moral law' at all.

Schopenhauer's ethical theory does not stand entirely under Kant's shadow, any more than his theory of knowledge or his aesthetics – yet the shadow is always present. Kant's ethics is an ethics of duty, and tries to formulate an imperative to which the actions of the ideally rational being must conform. Schopenhauer's, by contrast, is an ethics of compassion. It tries to explain the difference between good and bad in terms of a divergence of attitudes which individuals may take towards one another, and towards the world as a whole. Morality for Schopenhauer is not a matter of duty or of 'ought'; nor can it be founded in rationality. It is a matter of 'seeing the world aright', to use Wittgenstein's later phrase. But to reach his position Schopenhauer first has to argue with Kant in some detail.

The essay *On the Basis of Morality* contains a succinct and powerful discussion of Kantian ethics, in which Schopenhauer brings forward many objections, chief among them the objection that Kant's idea of an imperative, 'You ought', is a theological notion in disguise. The language in which Kant speaks here has biblical overtones, and, to the atheist Schopenhauer, the very idea of an absolute command either trades surreptitiously on the assumption of an absolute being who may issue it, or it is unfounded. When Kant later tries to show how ethics requires an idea of God, Schopenhauer is reminded of a conjuror who, to our great surprise, pulls out of the hat something which he had planted there all along (*B*, 57). On the other hand, if there is no God, we should not simply swallow the idea of an absolute, universal imperative in the first place.

To whom, in any case, would the Kantian imperative be addressed? Not to human beings as such, but to 'all rational beings'. Schopenhauer is again scathing:

> we know *reason* as the exclusive attribute of the human race, and are by no means entitled to think of it as existing outside that race, and to set up a *genus* called 'rational beings' differing from its sole species, 'man'.

Still less are we justified in laying down laws for such imaginary *rational beings in the abstract* . . . We cannot help suspecting that Kant here gave a thought to the dear little angels, or at any rate counted on their presence in the conviction of the reader. (*B*, 63-4)

Kant's moral imperative has to be issued to rational beings in the abstract, because his ethics sets out to be non-empirical, and to rest wholly on principles knowable a priori – that is to say, knowable in advance of experience. But this itself is something that should be queried, according to Schopenhauer. Practical morality – decision-making and judgement – is concerned with the actual conduct of individual human beings who occupy the empirical realm. This should also be the focus of the theoretical discussion which Schopenhauer calls 'morals'. He charges that Kant's moral imperative is by contrast purely formal, and so without any 'real substance' (*B*, 76).

What about the Kantian appeal to rationality? Schopenhauer points out that rational behaviour is not always morally good behaviour: 'Reasonable and vicious are quite consistent with each other, in fact, only through their union are great and far-reaching crimes possible' (*B*, 83). In other words, if one is evil, rationality will not make one any *less* evil; it may simply make one a more efficient and deadly exponent than an evil person who cannot think straight. Reason is instrumental, concerning the means towards some end which one has. An imperative will therefore motivate a rational being to action, only if he or she has an interest or end already in view. Since *human* beings are material, striving individuals who manifest the will to life, their ends tend to be egoistic. Egoism is the 'paymaster' required to cash out any formal imperative (*B*, 89): what will rationally motivate me to act in any particular case will be considerations about whether I can achieve *my* own ends.

One final criticism is perhaps worthy of mention. Schopenhauer is affronted by Kant's idea of the 'dignity of man' – our supposed 'unconditioned incomparable value' – and by the idea that human

Die

beiden Grundprobleme

der

behandelt

in zwei akademischen Preisschriften

von

Dr Arthur Schopenhauer,

Mitglied der Königl. Norwegischen Societät der Wissenschaften.

———

I. Ueber die Freiheit des menschlichen Willens, gekrönt
von der Königl. Norwegischen Societät der Wissenschaften,
zu Drontheim, am 26. Januar 1839.

II. Ueber das Fundament der Moral, nicht gekrönt von
der K. Dänischen Societät der Wissenschaften, zu Kopenhagen,
den 30. Januar 1840.

————————

Frankfurt am Main,

Joh. Christ. Hermann'sche Buchhandlung.

F. E. Suchsland.

1841.

10. Title page of *The Two Fundamental Problems of Ethics* beings must be treated as 'ends in themselves'. One ground for his criticism is that something can be a 'value' or 'end' only if it is the fulfilment of something specific that is willed. 'Unconditioned value' and 'end in itself' would in that case be disguised contradictions. More significantly, Schopenhauer finds this elevation of the human species at the expense of other animals 'revolting and abominable'. Other species are supposed to lack such dignity, and not to be ends in themselves, solely through lacking reason; but the consequence is that, in philosophical morals, animals

> are mere 'things', mere *means* to any ends whatsoever. They can therefore be used for vivisection, hunting, coursing, bull-fights, and horse racing, and can be whipped to death as they struggle along with heavy carts of stone. Shame on such a morality . . . that fails to recognize the eternal essence that exists in every living thing, and shines forth with inscrutable significance from all eyes that see the sun! (*B*, 96)

Schopenhauer sounds almost our contemporary here. At the same time, his lack of confidence in any special value attaching to humanity or to rationality is an important element in his pessimism. As we shall see, being an individual of the human species is neither a dignified nor a good thing as such.

Freedom and determinism

Schopenhauer believes that actions are caused by a combination of one's unchanging character and a motive occurring in one's consciousness. This is the basis of his claim that all actions are determined, and that, in one important sense, there is no freedom of the will. But his discussion of the issue, especially in its concentrated form in *On the Freedom of the Will*, is of considerable subtlety. As well as arguing for determinism, he makes an important distinction between different senses of 'freedom', and finishes with the reflection that the truth of determinism does not make us any less inclined to feel responsible for our actions – a fact which he rightly says still requires an explanation.

Schopenhauer brings to light a distinction, which is often overlooked, between freedom to will and freedom to act. Freedom to act is the ability to do something, if one wills to do it. This freedom can be removed by external obstacles to action, by constraining motives, laws or threats of various consequences if one acts, or by impairment of the subject's cognitive faculties. Being in prison, being at gunpoint, or having sustained brain-damage are, for example, all ways in which there can be some obstacle to one's doing what one wills. Schopenhauer accordingly lists physical freedom, moral freedom, and intellectual freedom as the three species of freedom to act. The deeper question, however, is whether I have any freedom to *will* this or that course of action. Schopenhauer arrives at his admirably straight answer to this question by examining the only two available sources of evidence: consciousness of ourselves and consciousness of things other than ourselves.

Consciousness of ourselves is powerless to tell us whether we could ever have willed otherwise than we did. In self-consciousness we are aware of doing what we want to do, by being aware of our action itself and of the motives that bring it about. But once I have chosen one course of action, say, going to Frankfurt, can I tell whether I *could* equally have chosen to go to Mannheim? The problem is this:

> Everyone's self-consciousness asserts very clearly that he can do what he wills. But since we can conceive of him as willing quite opposite actions, it follows that if he so wills he can also *do* the opposite. Now the untutored understanding confuses this with the proposition that he, in a given case, can also *will* the opposite, and calls this the freedom of the will. ... But whether in a given case he can *will* the one as well as the other ... calls for a deeper investigation than the one which mere self-consciousness could decide. (*F*, 23)

The question is not whether one can want or wish to do each of two opposite actions, but whether one could will them – remembering that (barring obstacles) willing is acting, for Schopenhauer. I went to Frankfurt, and I am aware that if it had been my will to go to Mannheim, I could have done that. The question is: could that have been my will? Schopenhauer's sensible answer is that, from examining my own knowledge of my actions and motives, I cannot decide this question.

On the other hand, if one looks at the causal relation between the external world and the subject who wills, one is bound to treat the case as one treats any other cause–effect relationship. I cannot regard myself alone as the one part of the world that is exempt from the principle of sufficient reason; so, if the state of affairs which caused me to go to Frankfurt were exactly repeated, it could only cause me to go to Frankfurt. It makes no difference that part of the cause is a process of rational deliberation. Schopenhauer contends that if my character and the motive – my representation of reality – were to remain the same, then I could not have willed otherwise. In this sense, there is no free will. We think we have it, but all that we have is the freedom to do what we will, with which it is so easily confused.

The argument is already cogent, but the way in which Schopenhauer caps it shows his peculiar skill as a philosophical writer. Imagine a man standing on the street at six o'clock in the evening, he says, musing on the following thoughts: 'The working day is over. Now I can go for a walk, or I can go to the club; I can also climb up the tower to see the sun set' – and so on – 'I also can run out of the gate, into the wide world, and never return. All of this is strictly up to me, in this I have complete freedom. But still I shall do none of these things now, but with just as free a will I shall go home to my wife.' Schopenhauer's comment?

This is exactly as if water spoke to itself: 'I can make waves (yes! in the sea during a storm), I can rush down hill (yes! in the river bed)' I can plunge

94

down foaming and gushing (yes! in the waterfall), I can rise freely as a
stream of water into the air (yes! in the fountain), I can, finally, boil away
and disappear (yes! at a certain temperature); but I am doing none of
these things now, and am voluntarily remaining quiet and clear water in
the reflecting pond. (F, 43)

After stating his case for determinism, however, Schopenhauer reserves
the right to a 'higher view'. 'For there is another fact of consciousness
which until now I have left completely aside', he says. 'This is the wholly
clear and certain feeling of the *responsibility* for what we do, of the
accountability for our actions, which rests on the unshakable certainty
that we ourselves are the doers of our deeds' (F, 93-4). As some
philosophers have said recently, the truth of determinism does not take
away this 'certain feeling' that we are accountable for our actions, that
they are in some sense 'up to us'.

Schopenhauer now turns to a distinction in Kant's ethics, namely that
between a person's empirical character and their intelligible character,
'one of the most beautiful and profound ideas brought forth by that
great mind, or indeed by men at any time' (F, 96). This is another aspect
of the backbone distinction between appearance and thing in itself with
which we have dealt all along:

> the empirical character, like the whole man, is a mere appearance as an
> object of experience, and hence bound to the forms of all appearance –
> time, space, and causality – and subject to their laws. On the other hand,
> the condition and the basis of this whole appearance . . . is his intelligible
> character, i.e. his will as thing in itself. It is to the will in this capacity that
> freedom, and to be sure even absolute freedom, that is, independence of
> the law of causality (as a mere form of appearances), properly belongs.
> (F, 97)

The basic idea is quite simple: if I cannot escape from causal necessity as
part of empirical reality, then an aspect of me that is beyond empirical

reality may do so. Schopenhauer points out that when we hold someone accountable we blame the person for his or her character, or for what he or she *is*, using actions merely as evidence for this. He suggests that I must be responsible for what I am – my intelligible character behind appearances, from which issue all my actions. Freedom is not eliminated, but moved out of the empirical realm.

Here Schopenhauer faces some serious problems. One is that, on his own view, my character is inborn and unchanging. In what sense can I then be responsible for being what I am? Another problem is that *I* seem to disappear from the world in itself. The thing in itself is not split up into individuals – a crucial claim throughout Schopenhauer's philosophy. '*My* will as thing in itself', my intelligible character, ought not to be separate from the world as whole; and so it is hard to see how I could be held responsible for 'what I am in myself'. Schopenhauer is right in saying that we do regard a person as responsible for actions, thinking of the person as their true source, regardless of their place in a causal chain of events. But, although his may be an acute diagnosis of the problem of free will, Schopenhauer's solution is not really credible.

Egoism and compassion

What then is the true basis of morals, according to Schopenhauer? The answer may be given in three stages. One concerns the single principle which, he claims, all moral actions conform to, namely: 'Injure no one; on the contrary, help everyone as much as you can' (which he gives in Latin: *Neminem laede, imo omnes quantum potes, juva*). The second stage of the answer is an attempt to explain the basic psychological attitude which alone can spur people on to moral actions, namely compassion or sympathy. Ultimately, however, the basis of morals is not reached until the third stage, in which we are given a metaphysical account of how the compassionate attitude is both possible and justified.

The '*Neminem laede*' principle can be broken into two parts: 'Injure no one' and 'Help everyone as much as you can'. Actions which conform to the first part Schopenhauer calls instances of voluntary justice, while those which conform to the second are instances of disinterested philanthropy, or 'loving-kindness' towards other human beings (and presumably towards animals too: in line with his earlier censure of Kant, Schopenhauer adduces the fact that we *do* feel compassion towards animals [*B*, 175–8]). No action except those of pure justice or philanthropy can count as having true moral worth (*B*, 138–9). Schopenhauer takes it as a premiss that such acts, however rare and surprising, are acknowledged to occur, and are universally regarded as being good. Examples range from self-sacrifice in battle to someone's returning a lost object which they could have kept without any consequences, or giving alms to a beggar when they stand to gain nothing from doing so. Justice and philanthropy both stem from compassion, which manifests itself either as pure concern to promote the well-being of another, or as pure distress at the suffering of another.

Every human being, according to Schopenhauer, has some element of compassion in their character (*B*, 192). But there are vast differences in the proportion of compassion with which we are endowed. Some are overflowing with it, some have virtually none in them. Schopenhauer thinks that only actions from compassion have moral worth, and that we judge primarily what a person is, using their actions merely as evidence. If we follow him in all this, we shall have to admit that some human beings are greatly more good than others, and that some, though they might occasionally act from compassion, are not good. Whether or not that is a problem, it pales into insignificance compared with the difficulty of explaining how, on his view, compassion is possible at all, and how it can be an incentive to action.

If some part of everyone's make-up is compassion, what is the rest? Schopenhauer's claim in full is this:

> Man's three fundamental ethical incentives, egoism, malice, and
> compassion, are present in everyone in different and incredibly unequal
> proportions. In accordance with them, motives will operate on man and
> actions will ensue. (B, 192)

Schopenhauer helps us with a succinct explanation of the three
incentives. Compassion is the incentive to seek the well-being of
another (or to alleviate their woe). Malice is the incentive to seek the
woe of another; egoism the incentive to seek one's own well-being. We
may wonder whether the logic of this triad is quite right: is not malice
really a kind of self-seeking, a kind of egoism? In Schopenhauer's
defence, the reply must be that some malice at least is not egoistic.
Much that we can set down as cruelty is done at the behest of one's own
gain in some form or other: it is then a means to an egoistic end. But
what Schopenhauer means by pure malice is something as exceptional
as pure philanthropy: the kind of depraved or 'devilish' action where the
agent sets aside his or her own well-being as an aim, simply in order to
harm someone else (B, 136) – what one might call disinterested malice.
The triad of egoism, malice, and compassion is thus a genuine
threesome, although many cruel and wicked actions do not arise from
malice proper.

Nevertheless it is the egoistic incentive that compassion most has to
contend with, because it is egoism that makes up the bulk of each
individual: 'The chief and fundamental incentive in man as in the animal
is *egoism*, that is, the craving for existence and well-being' (B, 131). Each
individual is a material organism in which will to life expresses itself:
hence striving for one's own ends is fundamental to each individual.
Indeed, so fundamental is it on Schopenhauer's theory that one must
wonder how compassionate action is possible at all. If action is always a
bodily striving of the individual towards some end of its own,
compassion, which is supposedly the only genuine moral incentive,
ought never to move any individual to action. Egoism is 'colossal' and
'natural':

every individual, completely vanishing and reduced to nothing in a boundless world, nevertheless makes himself the centre of the world, and considers his own existence and well-being before everything else. In fact, from the natural standpoint, he is ready for this to sacrifice everything else; he is ready to annihilate the world, in order to maintain his own self, that drop in the ocean, a little longer. This disposition is *egoism*, which is essential to everything in nature. (W1, 332)

Egoism 'towers over the world' (B, 132) to such an extent that, without the constraint of laws embodied in the state, individuals would be engaged in *bellum omnium contra omnes*, a war of all against all (B, 133). All this suggests that action motivated by pure concern for the well-being of others should be not only rare, but so contrary to our nature as to be impossible. Schopenhauer has to admit that compassion is one of the mysteries of ethics. His only choice is to say that compassion is a primitive anti-egoistic trait which, as a matter of sheer fact, is present in us. But how compassion can 'reside in human nature' (B, 149) is deeply mysterious given that the human being is a naturally egoistic expression of will to life.

The metaphysics of morals

The final stage of Schopenhauer's ethics, however, seeks to rest the compassionate attitude on a metaphysical foundation. Compassion turns out to reflect a view of oneself and the nature of reality which differs from that implicit in egoism, and is superior to it. Schopenhauer can thus say that compassion is a good thing not only because it tends to decrease the sum of suffering in the world, but because it embodies a truer metaphysical picture.

The initial thought is that it is possible for me to feel compassion only if 'to a certain extent I have identified myself with the other person, and in consequence the barrier between the I and the non-I is for the moment abolished' (B, 166). Schopenhauer takes rather literally the idea contained in 'compassion' or 'sympathy' (German *Mitleid*) that one person 'suffers with' another. Thought for my well-being has to yield its place in my motivation to thought for another's well-being; and it would be inexplicable how that could happen unless I could make the other's suffering and well-being intimately my own concern. Only if I share your suffering, in some sense feeling it as my own, can your well-being, or the alleviation of your woe, come to motivate me. To be compassionate, someone must, says Schopenhauer, 'make less of a distinction than do the rest between himself and others' (*B*, 204).

But now he can argue that the compassionate person is committed to a different metaphysical view:

> The *bad* man everywhere feels a thick partition between himself and everything outside him. The world to him is an *absolute non-I* and his relation to it is primarily hostile. ... The good character, on the other hand, lives in an external world that is homogeneous with his own true being. The others are not non-I for him, but an 'I once more'. His fundamental relation to everyone is, therefore, friendly; he feels himself intimately akin to all beings, takes an immediate interest in their weal and woe, and confidently assumes the same sympathy in them. (*B*, 211)

Which is the correct view of the world? The appearance/thing in itself dichotomy will tell us. From the point of view of the world of representation, governed by space and time which are the principle of individuation, reality consists of separate individuals, of which any moral agent is one. So the person who thinks 'Each individual is a being radically different from all others . . . everything else is non-I and foreign to me' (*B*, 210) is right about the world of appearance. But beneath this lies the world as thing in itself, which is not split up into individuals, but just is *the world* – whatever that ultimately is. So the supposedly more profound view is the one which considers individuation to be 'mere phenomenon' rather than ultimately part of reality. From this point of view, no one is distinct from anything else in the world, and so can recognize 'in *another* his own self, his own true inner nature' (*B*, 209). Schopenhauer's Indian thoughts come to the fore suddenly: the conception of the world as composed of separate individuals is *Mâyâ* – 'i.e. illusion, deception, phantasm, mirage' (*B*, 209), while knowledge of the deeper, more correct, non-individuating view is expressed in the Sanskrit *tat tvam asi*: this art thou (*B*, 210).

At first sight this idea seems so extreme as to expunge the possibility of compassion altogether. If I really believed that you were not distinct from me, the attitude with which I regarded you could only be a strange kind of egoism. Genuine compassion, on the other hand, surely presupposes belief in distinctness as a minimum condition. An even more graphic objection is that, if the world in itself is without individuation, it does not even contain *me*: it certainly does not contain me as this bodily, willing human being, nor does it contain the thinking 'I' that I regard myself as being from a subjective point of view. It is hard to see how the belief in the illusoriness of all individuals, including the individual which I am, could support a compassionate attitude between the individual that I am and the individual beggar to whom I give money.

But perhaps this is too simplistic a response. What Schopenhauer has recognized is the possibility of an attitude to the world which does not take one's existence as a particular individual to be of paramount significance: a 'universal standpoint' as opposed to a particular one (*W*2, 599–600). In order to adopt this standpoint, one need not abandon the belief in separate individuals altogether. Compassion is supposed to motivate actions which one must carry out as an individual, towards other individuals. What might ground such actions is the idea that, though individuals are separate, there is nothing of any fundamental importance about the individual which I am. If the beggar and I are both equal portions of the same underlying reality, equal manifestations of the same will to life, then from the point of view of the world as a whole, it is a matter of indifference whether my ends are promoted and the beggar's thwarted, or vice versa. This thought seems genuinely capable of grounding a compassionate outlook. The belief that I simply am not an individual separate from the rest of reality is not what does the work here; rather it is that, though being an individual (and naturally egoistic) thing in the world, my perspective does not always have to be one of identification with the individual that I am. As in Schopenhauer's account of aesthetic experience, I need not accept the natural standpoint of individuality as the one from which I must always regard things. In the next chapter we shall see that the individual's renunciation of his or her individuality not only makes aesthetic value and moral worth possible for Schopenhauer, but is the only attitude which can compensate for his or her existing at all.

Chapter 8
Existence and pessimism

Ineliminable suffering

> Awakened to life out of the night of unconsciousness, the will finds itself
> as an individual in an endless and boundless world, among innumerable
> individuals, all striving, suffering, and erring; and, as if through a
> troubled dream, it hurries back to the old unconsciousness. Yet till then
> its desires are unlimited, its claims inexhaustible, and every satisfied
> desire gives birth to a new one. No possible satisfaction in the world
> could suffice to still its craving, set a final goal to its demands, and fill
> the bottomless pit of its heart. In this connexion, let us now consider
> what as a rule comes to man in satisfactions of any kind; it is often
> nothing more than the bare maintenance of this very existence,
> extorted daily with unremitting effort and constant care in conflict with
> misery and want, and with death in prospect. Everything in life
> proclaims that earthly happiness is destined to be frustrated, or
> recognized as an illusion. The grounds for this lie deep in the very
> nature of things. (W2, 573)

The Fourth Book of *The World as Will and Representation* is its austere
final movement. Schopenhauer's style matches the greater seriousness
of the discussion (W1, 271), which, together with the topics in ethics we
have already looked at, addresses – to use a hackneyed phrase – the
human condition itself. Few writers have the insight and eloquence to

make a philosophically interesting contribution in this area, but Schopenhauer is undoubtedly one of them.

Schopenhauer looks around the world and finds it full of suffering – frustration, tedium, pain, and misery. It might be thought that this is just a matter of personal propensity. Someone else might point out the occurrence of good fortune, innocent joy, contentment, and reward for honest toil – so is not Schopenhauer merely carrying out a highly selective inventory? If so, his pessimism would be superficial and gratuitous. But this is not the case. Whether we agree with him or not, he has arguments for far-reaching conclusions about the value that can attach to human existence. It must contain suffering, and cannot be preferable to non-existence. It would even have been better for reality not to have existed. These claims make Schopenhauer a pessimist in a philosophically interesting sense.

The first point is that suffering is ineliminably present in the existence of any human individual. As material, living creatures, our ordinary existence is such that we must strive towards ends. But, Schopenhauer argues, a being who strives, and who is conscious of his or her ends and of whether they are fulfilled, is a being who suffers. Part of this can be understood in terms of egoism. Among a multitude of individuals, each of whom must strive in order to exist, conflicts of ends will occur, and, barring the mysterious intervention of compassion, suffering will result. Since compassion is not ubiquitous, nor even widespread, one's life as a human individual among others will be very likely to contain episodes in which one suffers, and episodes in which one brings about suffering.

However, willing itself is closely intertwined with suffering in another way. First, willing could not spring from a state of total sufficiency and contentment. A being strives only if it experiences a lack or deficiency, and experiencing a lack is already a form of suffering. Secondly, in the course of events one does not attain some of the ends for which one strives. If one does not achieve an end, one's original lack is prolonged, which, together with the consciousness of not achieving one's end, is further suffering. Perhaps we can imagine a being that was always successful in its striving – but that is of little help to Schopenhauer. For what happens when we achieve an end towards which our striving has been directed? The resulting state is called satisfaction or happiness; but, he claims, this state is of value only relative to the deficiency which it removes. Satisfaction can occur only in a being that has suffered, and it has any value only relative to some particular episode of suffering. Schopenhauer puts the point by saying that satisfaction is negative, and pain positive. Pain is something which we feel, but satisfaction is an absence; to be satisfied is simply to return to neutral by wiping out a felt deficiency. And the mere state of feeling no deficiencies, and so having nothing to strive for, has no positive value in its own terms. If it continues for any length of time it is simply boredom, which Schopenhauer often mentions as one of the pervasive features of life. Finally, the attainment of ends never makes striving cease altogether. 'Every satisfied desire gives birth to a new one': whatever striving of ours is successful, we shall soon continue to strive for further ends, and hence to suffer further. Therefore, striving cannot eliminate suffering as such. While we exist, nothing we can undertake to *do* will stop us from willing, or, therefore, from having to suffer.

It is important for Schopenhauer that life's containing suffering is not redeemed by suffering's having any positive point. Many lives, as a matter of fact, strike a balance between suffering and contentment which suffices to make them bearable:

> This is the life of almost all men; they will, they know what they will, and they strive after this with enough success to protect them from despair, and enough failure to preserve them from boredom and its consequences. (W1, 327)

But if we consider simply that there is suffering, and ask whether existence containing suffering is something good, we cannot say that suffering is redeemed by some good over and above existence itself. If suffering in general is to be redeemed, it must be by its being simply good to exist as a human individual, come what may. And, as we shall see, that is something which Schopenhauer denies outright. But so far, if we accept Schopenhauer's argument, we can at least conclude that the happiness attainable by any human being must be bound up with suffering. To imagine an existence free of suffering is to imagine an existence that is not that of a human individual.

Death

What attitude should any of us take towards the most obvious fact about our existence – that it will cease? We do tend to fear death, not on any good rational ground, according to Schopenhauer, but because we are manifestations of will to life: a 'boundless attachment to life' is inborn in us as much as it is in all animals (W2, 465). We might be right to fear dying, if that process involved pain, but then the object of fear would be pain, rather than being dead. Schopenhauer presents a couple of familiar arguments for the view that fear of being dead is irrational. One is the argument from symmetry: we did not exist for an infinite time before birth, and that is a matter of indifference to us, so we ought to regard similarly our not existing again. The other is Epicurus' argument that precisely *because* it involves our non-existence, death should not be feared: to something that does not exist, it cannot matter that it does not exist.

Schopenhauer does, however, offer a more positive consolation. He accepts that death is the cessation of the individual human being, but maintains that this is not the only way in which it should be regarded. The opinion of many in contemporary Europe vacillates between the view of death as absolute annihilation and the notion of immortality. But both opinions are 'equally false' (W2,464). This becomes apparent from a 'higher standpoint' which once again exploits the distinction between thing in itself and phenomenon. The individual that I am is merely part of the world of phenomena. It occupies certain portions of space for a certain time, after which it ceases to exist. From the point of view of the individual, death is annihilation, and it would be absolute annihilation of me, if this particular phenomenal individual were all that I am. However, if I am also something in myself, outside all time and change, then death cannot be my end:

> the greatest equivocation really lies in the word 'I' . . . According as I understand this word, I can say: 'Death is my entire end'; or else: 'This my personal phenomenal appearance is just as infinitely small a part of my true inner nature as I am of the world.' (W2, 491)

'My true inner nature' here must refer to the same thing as 'the world', because reality *in itself* is not subject to any individuation. The 'higher standpoint' thus yields the thought that I am the world; and, thinking this, one can take the supposedly consoling view that the ephemeral individual to which 'I' usually refers is really not worth worrying about.

Once again Schopenhauer is trying to loosen the hold of the usual identification which we make of ourselves with an individual. The world manifests itself as me here and now, but after I cease to exist, the same world will manifest itself in the same way as other individuals of the same species, each of which will find itself as the subject of consciousness, refer to itself as 'I', pursue its ends, experience suffering and satisfaction, and cease to exist in turn. Reality in itself, I am supposed to think, is indifferent between one such manifestation of will and another. Nature itself does not grieve over the destruction of any particular part of itself, and will carry on existing without me. If I share with all other phenomena the same 'inner nature', then the very core of what I am carries on, regardless of the passing of phenomena. Indeed, 'carries on' is a misleading way to put Schopenhauer's point. Reality in itself is eternal in the sense of timelessness. I have my 'now', and every other phenomenon that was or will be has its time, which for it is equally a 'now'. But from the point of view of reality in itself, time is an illusion.

Hence the phenomenal fact that some particular thing will not exist later than now is not a fact about reality in itself.

Two concerns arise here: that this may not be convincing as an exercise in metaphysics, and that it might fail to be consoling even if it were thus convincing. The notion that the thing in itself is undifferentiated and timeless stems from Schopenhauer's idealist doctrine of space and time, and may well be questioned if we have doubts about that doctrine. The really troublesome point, however, is the idea that *I* am somehow present in the timeless, undifferentiated world. Schopenhauer has previously told us that 'I' refers to the material, striving, human being, and to the pure subject of consciousness which we find ourselves as, and which would not exist were it not for the human being with his or her bodily organs. But how could anything to which 'I' refers remain if the human being ceased to exist, taking with it the subject's consciousness? What we said when discussing the compassionate person's non-egoistic world-view applies again to the higher perspective on death: it is impossible to find *myself* in the picture of ultimate reality that it requires.

The question whether Schopenhauer's higher view of death could be consoling is a difficult one. He tries to inculcate the thought that one's own death has no great significance in the order of things. But if one accepted his reasons for taking this attitude, ought one not to think that one's life has just as little significance? And is that a consoling thought? Schopenhauer appears to think so:

> death is the great opportunity no longer to be I . . . Dying is the moment
> of that liberation from the one-sidedness of an individuality which does
> not constitute the innermost kernel of our true being, but is rather to be
> thought of as a kind of aberration thereof. (W2, 507–8)

In fact, Schopenhauer recognizes two distinct outlooks for which his view of death might be a consolation. The first, the *affirmation of the will to life*, is the outlook of someone who would, as it were, stand on the earth with 'firm, strong bones':

> A man ... who found satisfaction in life and took perfect delight in it; who desired, in spite of calm deliberation, that the course of his life as he had hitherto experienced it should be of endless duration or of constant recurrence; and whose courage to face life was so great that, in return for life's pleasures, he would willingly and gladly put up with all the hardships and miseries to which it is subject. (*W1*, 283-4)

This person could be consoled by Schopenhauer's doctrine of our indestructibility by death: 'Armed with the knowledge we confer on him, he would look with indifference at death hastening towards him on the wings of time. He would consider it as a false illusion' (*W1*, 284). Such a person would think that living as an individual is fine, but that the cessation of this life is powerless to detract from that.

Schopenhauer suggests that suicide stems from this same attitude of affirmation towards life. The explanation of this (which seems at first bizarre) is as follows: if I regard the pleasures of life as of positive value, despite its pains, I always run the risk that life's pains will come to outweigh its pleasures. If I continue to want life for its potential positive side, but come to believe that only suffering is available, the solution is to stop living. However:

> Far from being denial of the will, suicide is a phenomenon of the will's strong affirmation. For denial has its essential nature in the fact that the pleasures of life, not its sorrows, are shunned. The suicide wills life, and is dissatisfied merely with the conditions on which it has come to him. Therefore he gives up by no means the will to life, but merely life, since he destroys the individual phenomenon. (*W1*, 398)

Thus the character who wills the endless recurrence of his or her life (from whom, again, Nietzsche seems to have learned something), and the character who ends his or her life when suffering becomes too great, really take one and the same stance of affirmation. Both, though, would be missing something else: they would not have come to know the truth as Schopenhauer sees it, that 'constant suffering is essential to all life' (*W1*, 283). The alternative outlook, which encompasses this truth, consists in the *denial of the will to life*. Recognizing that suffering pervades any existence as an individual manifestation of will to life, and that achieving ends can never be divorced from suffering, this attitude ceases to look for any positive value in the life of the individual human being, even from its passing moments of satisfaction. This provides a unique attitude to death:

> to die willingly, to die gladly, to die cheerfully, is the prerogative of the resigned, of him who gives up and denies the will to life. . . . He willingly gives up the existence that we know; what comes to him instead of it is in our eyes *nothing*, because our existence in reference to that one is *nothing*. The Buddhist faith calls that existence *Nirvana*, that is to say, extinction. (*W2*, 508)

Denial of the will

The will to life must be denied – 'if salvation is to be attained from an existence like ours' (*W1*, 405). Salvation is a religious doctrine, and Schopenhauer is keen to link his philosophical discussion with Christianity, Brahmanism, and Buddhism, claiming that the core of all these religions, leaving aside mythical trappings and recent doctrinal accretions, is really the same. Even God is not to the point: the philosophical import is available to an atheist quite as much as to a theist (*W1*, 385), and is that we must renounce, or say No to, our nature as human beings, if we are to find true value in existing. The real self is the will to life (*W2*, 606), and since this is also what must be denied, salvation lies in self-denial or self-renunciation. 'In fact', he says, 'nothing else can be stated as the aim of our existence except the knowledge that it would be better for us not to exist' (*W2*, 605).

In 'denial of the will to life', one turns against the particular manifestation of will to life found in oneself, which means turning against the body, and against one's own individuality. Thus one ceases, as much as possible, to strive for one's own egoistic ends, ceases to avoid suffering or to seek pleasure, ceases to desire propagation of the species, or any sexual gratification – in short, one looks down on that willing part of nature which one is, and withdraws from one's identification with it. Such an apparently unpalatable state is made to seem worthy of attainment by Schopenhauer's elevated prose:

> we can infer how blessed must be the life of a man whose will is silenced not for a few moments, as in the enjoyment of the beautiful, but for ever, indeed completely extinguished, except for the last glimmering spark that maintains the body and is extinguished with it. Such a man who, after many bitter struggles with his own nature, has at last completely conquered, is then left only as pure knowing being, as the undimmed mirror of the world. Nothing can distress or alarm him any more; nothing can any longer move him; for he has cut all the thousand threads of willing which hold us bound to the world, and which as craving, fear, envy, and anger drag us here and there in constant pain. (W1, 390)

> Then, instead of the restless pressure and effort; instead of the constant transition from desire to apprehension and from joy to sorrow; instead of the never-satisfied and never-dying hope that constitutes the life-dream of the man who wills, we see that peace that is higher than all reason, that ocean-like calmness of the spirit, that deep tranquillity, that unshakable confidence and serenity, whose mere reflection in the countenance, as depicted by Raphael and Correggio, is a complete and certain gospel. Only knowledge remains; the will has vanished. (W1, 411)

Despite its kinship with the tranquil contemplation of the beautiful, the denial of the will is not to be reached by an aesthetic route. It is reached first by a saintly life, one whose justice and philanthropy arise from the insight that egoism, individuation, and the whole phenomenal world are a kind of delusion. The supposed knowledge that all things are identical at the level of the 'in itself' leads to the total surrender of egoism, and to the embracing of all suffering as one's own. This 'knowledge of the whole' then becomes the '*quieter* of all and every willing' (*W1*, 379), and turns the will against its natural state of self-affirmation. Another, secondary route to the same state is through suffering itself. This is more common, according to Schopenhauer, since the saintly life is not only rare, but extremely hard to sustain in the face of the allurements of the will (*W1*, 392). There are those, however, in real life or in tragic art, whose own individual pain is of such duration or intensity that their will to life is broken. Then, as a 'gleam of silver that suddenly appears from the purifying flame of suffering', the state of salvation may arrive in which they renounce all their desires, rise above themselves and above suffering in a state of 'inviolable peace, bliss and sublimity' (*W1*, 392–3).

Schopenhauer points to numerous practices and experiences which he thinks bear out his descriptions of self-renunciation:

> Quietism, i.e. the giving up of all willing, asceticism, i.e. intentional mortification of one's own will, and mysticism, i.e. consciousness of the identity of one's own inner being with that of all things, or with the kernel of the world, stand in the closest connexion, so that whoever professes one of them is gradually led to the acceptance of the others, even against his intention. Nothing can be more surprising than the agreement among the writers who express those teachings, in spite of the greatest difference of their age, country, and religion. (*W2*, 613)

The ascetic, not content with willing the well-being of others, actively seeks to counter the ends of the will as it expresses itself in the body. ('One's own woe' is thus a fourth *incentive* to action, to be set alongside those of egoism, malice, and compassion [*W2*, 607].) Schopenhauer describes the ascetic thus: 'His body, healthy and strong, expresses the sexual impulse through the genitals, but he denies the will, and gives the lie to the body' (W1, 380). Voluntary abstention from sexual activity – that most powerful manifestation of will to life – is accompanied by intentional poverty, non-avoidance of injury or ignominy from others, fasting, self-castigation, and self-torture. Since all these occurrences are pursued as deliberate ends, asceticism cannot be identical with total will-lessness. The latter must occur unpredictably as the 'sudden gleam of silver' arising out of suffering; one can deliberately engineer suffering, but true salvation does not come about by intention or design.

Mysticism, meanwhile, is simply 'consciousness of the identity of one's own inner being with that of all things'. Schopenhauer claims to have arrived at a philosophical delineation of the state which mystics achieve in subjective experience. But since this experience cannot be communicated, he arrives at the limits of philosophy:

> when my teaching reaches its highest point, it assumes a *negative* character, and so ends with a negation. Thus it can speak here only of what is denied or given up. . . . Now it is precisely here that the mystic proceeds positively, and therefore, from this point, nothing is left but mysticism. (W2, 612)

Schopenhauer's book, having begun with the words 'The world . . .', does indeed end with ' – Nothing'. The phenomenal world is negated by those whose will has turned against it, and they embrace sheer nothingness in return; but then, from their altered point of view, the whole of this world can be set at nought. Having given up placing any positive value in the human round of happiness and suffering, the will-less subject finds a new value in the very rejection of what has ordinary human value.

However sympathetic or unsympathetic we may be to Schopenhauer's final doctrine, we must surely worry whether it is really coherent at all. We have often enough questioned whether I can think of *myself* as

113

existing in a world deprived of all differentiation between individuals. But, even setting that aside, someone might ask: how can I acquiesce in a tranquil vision of my identity with the kernel of the world, if that kernel is the detested will to life, the very thing which it is so desirable for me to escape? There is, however, a reply to this worry. We must not forget Schopenhauer's distinction between knowing and willing. To *know* the whole world as an all-pervading, purposeless will to life is not the same as colluding with that will as it expresses itself in one's own body – it is not the same as willing on behalf of this particular individual. Salvation is achieved by knowledge for Schopenhauer, but not by knowledge that any good state of affairs obtains. To see the world as a whole from which I am not distinct is of value because it liberates me from the treadmill of striving, happiness, and suffering – but not because I come to understand the world as a good thing. The world is not a good thing, and nor am I, for Schopenhauer. But some value can be salvaged if I stand back and know the terrible place from a universal standpoint, rather than carrying on willing in unquestioning identification with one small part of it.

A final concern about the denial of the will is whether it is always bound to be an act of will. If I have a choice whether to affirm or deny my will to life, then, at some higher level, I must be willing to deny the will. This would not be a contradiction if the 'higher' willing, which discriminates between affirmation and denial, was of a kind not subordinate to the will to life: I could then decide at will to deny my will to life. But if Schopenhauer were to think that all willing is a form of will to life, and that the denial of will to life is something I undertake at will, then his position would be quite incoherent. The best resolution of this problem is to say that denial of the will simply occurs in a subject, and is not a consciously undertaken act. One's natural compassion for every being, or the degree of one's suffering, overcome one's egoism to such an extent that it becomes impossible to strive any longer for the ends that arise out of one's own parochial existence. His other description of this is 'the will to life turning against itself'. At the end of *The World as Will and Representation* he writes not of 'those who have denied the will', but of 'those in whom the will has turned and denied itself' (*W1*, 412). It is important that the agency here is not straightforwardly *mine*. Just as it is not I who originally throw myself into life, so it is not I who turn against the will to life. The 'agent' here is the will to life, which turns against itself. So denial of the will really is *not* an act of will of the person in whom it happens. However, Schopenhauer sometimes writes as if it were. Those in whom the will has turned must constantly 'struggle' against affirmation of the will, which is the body's natural state; they must 'strive with all their might to keep to this path by self-imposed renunciations of every kind' (*W1*, 391). The will to life within in me is recalcitrant, and reverts to affirming itself, even if it has previously been broken by saintliness or intense suffering, so here is a case where *I* must continue to will its denial after all.

Pessimism

Schopenhauer's philosophical pessimism resides in two connected theses: that for each individual it would have been better not to have been born, and that the world as a whole is the worst of all possible worlds. The argument for the first starts from the point that, for the ordinary, striving human being, life must contain suffering, and from the claim that all satisfaction is purely of negative value, being the cessation of suffering. Schopenhauer moves from here to the idea that no satisfaction achievable within human existence can compensate for the suffering that it must also contain. It is as if, in the balance, no satisfaction can weigh anything at all by comparison with any suffering, however small. The mere existence of evil in the world makes it something whose non-existence is preferable to its existence – we should wish not only not to have come into existence ourselves, but that this world in which we must suffer had not come about (*W2*, 576). All in all, our condition is 'something that it were better should not be' (*W2*, 577).

Now this argument is not one that we have to accept. It is quite plausible that our life has no purpose, that it must contain suffering, and that no satisfactions can ever expunge the evil of any single pain; in this sense the line Schopenhauer quotes from Petrarch, '*mille piacer' non vagliono un tormento*' – 'a thousand pleasures do not compensate for one pain' (*W2*, 576), is correct. Also, it may be true that existence is *not guaranteed* to be better than non-existence. And if, as Schopenhauer claims – again with some plausibility – 'nine-tenths of mankind live in constant conflict with want, always balancing themselves with difficulty and effort on the brink of destruction' (*W2*, 584), then the total of individual lives that are better than non-existence may be much smaller than we like to think. Still it does not follow that everyone should consider their actual existence worse than non-existence. The crucial premiss needed for this is that *any* suffering contained in a life makes non-existence preferable to it. But this step commits us to thinking that seventy years of contentment are rendered worthless by a single episode of pain – and that is surely incredible. We should question more strenuously the idea that all satisfaction is negative – the idea that while pain is *felt*, satisfaction is a mere restitution of neutrality. It is true that however many parts of one's life are happy, they do not take away the pain of the parts in which one suffers. But it should be equally true that the mere fact of suffering does not take away the value of the parts in which one does not suffer, which may happen to be quite numerous.

Schopenhauer is scathing about optimism, the view that this is the best of all possible worlds – 'The absurdity is glaring!' (*W2*, 581). His strongest attack is the argument that this is rather the worst of all possible worlds, which goes as follows: 'Take "possible" to mean "what can actually exist and last". Then, since "this world is arranged as it had to be if it were to be capable of continuing with great difficulty to exist" (*W2*, 583), we can see that a worse world than this could not continue to exist. Therefore, this is the worst world that is possible.' This is a curious argument. Schopenhauer cites a number of pieces of evidence for the claim that the world is continuing to exist only with great difficulty.

Nine-tenths of the human race live on the margins of extinction, many species have entirely disappeared, a very small change in temperature or the composition of the atmosphere would extinguish life altogether, the planet could easily be destroyed by collisions within the solar system, or by the forces beneath its own crust. So perhaps there are many possible worlds that are more remote from catastrophe than the present one – and if so, it may be salutary to be informed of that. But we can clearly imagine many changes distinctly for the worse in this world which would fall short of destroying it or its inhabitants. Many people nowadays believe the environment is becoming gradually less and less favourable for life. But if Schopenhauer were right, this view would be untenable: the end of the world would have to be as nigh now as it ever could be – and there appears no reason to accept this extreme view.

Schopenhauer's arguments for these extreme pessimist doctrines therefore fail to convince. However, his pessimism succeeds in advancing something less extreme and wholly believable, which is this: to think that we are *meant* not to suffer, that we somehow deserve happiness, or that the world owes us the fulfilment of our purposes, is a mistake – as is also the belief that being alive is simply a good a thing, whatever it brings. His protracted, moving discussions of the vanity or worthlessness (*Nichtigkeit*) of life enable us to escape from these optimistic delusions into a view which is harder, but arguably more humane: that life itself has no purpose, that suffering is always part of it, and that its end may sometimes be welcomed.

Despite this, it is sometimes suggested that Schopenhauer is not in the end a genuine pessimist at all. For it is not as if he really thinks that no value is ever attainable in life. Aesthetic contemplation, artistic genius, a life of philanthropy and justice, asceticism, and renunciation of the will, all are supreme values awaiting some human individuals, at least. The individual who escapes from the will achieves nothing less than 'salvation', which seems to be a state whose value is unassailable. All of this is true; but it conflicts with 'pessimism' only if you think pessimism is the view that nothing is of any value at all. It does not conflict with Schopenhauer's views that non-existence would have been preferable and that the world is the worst possible world. The values of will-lessness are genuine, but only by being, according to Schopenhauer, some amelioration of the worst situation possible. Someone might object that a worse world still would be one in which even the salvation of will-less resignation was not open to us. But Schopenhauer's reply would be that in that case existence would be so intolerable that no one who really understood its nature would be able to endure it. It would, in that sense, not be a possible existence.

Finally, even Schopenhauer's notion of salvation must itself be called pessimistic in a definite sense, if we consider that the only value worthy of the name in his scheme of things depends upon self-renunciation. Resignation and aesthetic tranquillity are achieved by an attitude of detachment from the human individual that strives for life, and from the whole tapestry of ends that are woven into life. If this living individual remains *what I am* in the world of representation, and will to life *what I am* in myself – no immaterial soul, no rational essence, no part of any divine plan – then *what I am* is not only worthless, but is the very obstacle that must be broken down before true value is glimpsed. To feel the full weight of Schopenhauer's *solution* to the problem of existence is thus to encounter a kind of self-loathing in which dwells the deepest pessimism of all.

Chapter 9
Schopenhauer's influence

Schopenhauer regarded himself as building a philosophical system which unfolded a 'single thought' (*W1*, xii). But the system, which is vulnerable to many criticisms, has not usually been the basis of his appeal. His lasting importance as a philosopher rests more on his manner of unfettered probing and blunt questioning, on his demolition of traditional certainties and on the new insecurities he confronts. The old ideas of the immortal soul, the divine purpose, and the dignity of man have died for Schopenhauer, and should not be revived. The human species is a part of nature, and rationality gives it no especially elevated status. The human individual is embodied and restlessly active, an animal who strives and suffers, whose core is sexuality and egoism. The identity of the individual becomes problematic through and through. Our mind is that of an organism adapted to the ends of living, and is split between the conscious, knowing, and seemingly unworldly self with which we try to identify, and the unconscious, natural will which seems alien but is truly what drives us on. Life has no purpose. Being ourselves is not something which has any positive value. Schopenhauer argues himself into a predicament in which existence itself is a problem, and then presents the exceptions of genius and saintliness, aesthetic experience and the submergence of individuality, as the only ways of salvaging value. Such uncomfortable, challenging thoughts represent his distinctive contribution to modern culture.

Although there has never really been a Schopenhauerian school of philosophy, his influence on the history of thought has been both great and varied. In the late nineteenth and early twentieth centuries he was at the forefront of European culture: his books were widely read, provided the material for many academic dissertations and published treatises, and were seized upon with enthusiasm by intellectuals and artists. He had some philosophical followers, but was perhaps more notable for attracting people who fell in love with his writing, turned over or wrestled with his thoughts, and then put them to their own creative use. In the 1850s Wagner fell under the Schopenhauerian spell, which became a major stimulant in the writing of *Tristan and Isolde* in particular. In the 1860s something similar happened to Nietzsche and to Tolstoy; in the 1880s and 1890s he was read by Thomas Hardy, Thomas Mann, and Marcel Proust, and in the 1900s by the young Wittgenstein. We find characters in *Buddenbrooks* and *À la Recherche du temps perdu* who read Schopenhauer, or discuss reading him; and he is mentioned in *Tess of the d'Urbervilles*. In all, there are many more notable artworks than can be catalogued here which bear the stamp of Schopenhauer's thinking, some directly, some more obliquely. The list of artists who became involved with his philosophy could continue for example, with Mahler, Richard Strauss, Turgenev, Lawrence, Beckett, and Borges.

Schopenhauer's appeal cannot be divorced from his own stature as a literary writer. His beautiful prose and his grasp of structure and drama – every step in the narrative marked by a powerful image and timed for maximum effect – make the transition from philosophical system to novel or opera stage almost as smooth as it could be. No single doctrine occupied all these writers and musicians equally, but the strongest impressions were undoubtedly made by his aesthetic theory, his philosophy of music, his recognition of the unconscious, his treatment of the overpowering sexual drive, his pessimism, and his questioning of the value of human existence. In some ways, it is strange that the period of Schopenhauer's most intense influence does not stretch much beyond the 1920s, into the decades when many of those we have mentioned had themselves become well-established cultural figures. This time of frustrated strivings in the economic sphere, when the futility of the First World War was compounded by yet more agonies, and widespread interest in psychoanalysis was changing people's views about the human personality – was this not Schopenhauer's true era? Yet by the middle of this century he was not such a well-known writer, one main reason being that none of the main streams of contemporary philosophy paid him any real attention.

Of those who succumbed to Schopenhauer, the earliest, Wagner and Nietzsche, seem to have been the most deeply affected, and it is in the understanding of these two that an exploration of the link with Schopenhauer is of most help. Wagner was no philosopher, and he sometimes confessed that, despite his constant re-readings, he was struggling to make out what was going on in Schopenhauer's work. Clearly the idea of music as the direct expression of the strivings of the will was one that spoke to him, but so did the idea of the denial of the will. He wrote in a letter to Liszt 'I have . . . found a sedative which has finally helped me to sleep at night; it is the sincere and heartfelt yearning for death: total unconsciousness, complete annihilation, the end of all dreams – the only ultimate redemption.' Wagner clearly felt that Schopenhauer's doctrine crystallized some of his own insights, and gave him a fresh outlook on his own existing work: 'Now at last I could understand my *Wotan*.' He comes closest to Schopenhauer's actual philosophy in his operas when the characters Tristan and Isolde express their deep longing to cease existing as individuals. The capacity of erotic love to overpower the individual is also one of Schopenhauer's themes, of course. Wagner, however, contrives to make the longing for non-existence turn into the climax of erotic love, instead of the complete negation of it which Schopenhauer calls for – in other words, even at his moment of supreme debt to the philosopher, he does not exactly follow him.

One of the things that brought Wagner together with the young

Nietzsche was their devotion to Schopenhauer, whom they had discovered independently. Even though Nietzsche had also experienced a kind of emotional 'conversion' to Schopenhauer's philosophy, his relationship with it was to be quite different. In his first publication, *The Birth of Tragedy*, Nietzsche uses the pair of symbolic deities Apollo and Dionysus to account for the awesome artistic achievement of Greek tragedy. Apollo stands for the beautiful dream-like image of the individual hero, Dionysus for the terrifying but intoxicating glimpse into the cruel world underlying individuation, which will destroy the hero. In attempting to explain this pair of symbols, he calls on Schopenhauer's distinction between representation and will. Although the book is a unique outpouring, much of which has little directly to do with Schopenhauer (as Nietzsche himself later commented), his reading of Schopenhauer was decisive in providing the shape and the impulse of it.

However, it is what happened later that gives Schopenhauer a greater significance for Nietzsche. He turned away from his former 'master', to the extent of saying that he 'went wrong everywhere'. As Nietzsche's own philosophy developed, Schopenhauer continued to be a guiding star of a special kind – the one to steer away from. In *On the Genealogy of Morality* he diagnoses Schopenhauer's doctrines as outlets for his own personality, saying in particular that the elevation of aesthetic tranquillity shows Schopenhauer's relief at escaping from his own abhorred sexual impulses; moreover 'he would have become ill, become a *pessimist* (for he was not one, however much he desired it), if deprived of his enemies, of Hegel, of woman, of sensuality and the whole will to existence, to persistence.' Perhaps – but what would Nietzsche have become without his Schopenhauer, his convenient summation of errors? He has already told us in the Preface: 'What was at stake was the *value* of morality – and over this I had to come to terms almost exclusively with my great teacher Schopenhauer.'

Nietzsche is very much concerned with the loss of value. He agrees with Schopenhauer that existence must contain suffering, and is basically without a point. But he revolts against the idea of renunciation and asceticism as a way to salvation. Plumbing the depths of the Schopenhauerian vision is a necessary step, but there must be an alternative to the 'life-denying' attitude of seeking to escape from the will and despising the individual material being that one is. Nietzsche's proposed solution is that of a creative self-affirmation ('Become who you are!'), embracing one's pain and even one's cruelty as true parts of oneself. His notion of the will to power, based more than verbally on Schopenhauer's 'will to life', attempts to supplant the latter as a description of the fundamental drive that organizes human behaviour, and, in some way, the whole universe. Will to power is not primarily a political doctrine, but an attempt to find an explanation of human behaviour, cognition, and cultural beliefs by positing an underlying tendency towards increase and mastery, both over the world and over oneself. Though he repudiates Schopenhauer's metaphysical doctrine of the thing in itself, and seeks to discredit philosophical metaphysics altogether, Nietzsche's notion of will to power shows striking parallels with Schopenhauer's conception of the will. In particular, the idea that will to power can be both conscious and unconscious, that it has an organic basis in the individual and that it is omnipresent, make it appropriate to call it a successor to Schopenhauer's doctrine.

While Schopenhauer is in the forefront of Nietzsche's critique of philosophers, many of the methods for that critique have also been suggested by Schopenhauer. For example, Nietzsche's view that metaphysical doctrines and beliefs about ethical values do not derive from 'pure' reasoning, but are always informed, covertly, by the need to come to terms with suffering and the will to master oneself or one's surroundings, clearly has its origins in Schopenhauer's doctrine that the will shapes our intellectual processes. Schopenhauer's idea that the world is structured by the mind of a particular species of living organism is reflected in Nietzsche's conviction that there are no absolute truths or values, only perspectives and fabrications that help us to cope with life. Schopenhauer also, of course, provides the most naked instance of the ascetic ideal which Nietzsche sees as underlying so much of Western culture – 'Man would rather will *nothingness* than *not* will.' Aside from such doctrinal influences, Nietzsche's writing displays its involvement with Schopenhauer often in fine-grained detail. He will appropriate Schopenhauer's nuances of voice and terminology even at the moment of greatest divergence from his doctrines. To read Nietzsche without a knowledge of Schopenhauer is to lose a recurring subtext and one of the key points of orientation in his often bewildering progress.

Among Nietzsche's contemporaries, philosophical interest in Schopenhauer was widespread. He was commonly studied as an important successor to Kant, and philosophers who were significant in their day, such as Hans Vaihinger and Nietzsche's friend the orientalist and metaphysician Paul Deussen, produced new systems which took off from Schopenhauer's. In the twentieth century he was highly thought of by members of the Frankfurt School who were dissatisfied with the optimism of orthodox Marxism, in particular Max Horkheimer. However, it is fair to say that to date the only major philosopher apart from Nietzsche to be influenced by Schopenhauer has been Wittgenstein. Wittgenstein, like Nietzsche, did not come across Schopenhauer's works in an academic setting. He read them as part of the stock of ideas with which Viennese high society was furnished (an illustrative little detail is that Gustav Mahler, another 'disciple', while staying at the Wittgenstein family house a few years earlier, had given Bruno Walter Schopenhauer's complete works as a present). In fact, not to have read Schopenhauer would have been the odd thing for a young person from a cultured family such as Wittgenstein's.

Wittgenstein's earliest philosophical work, leading up to the *Tractatus*, seems at first sight to have little in common with Schopenhauer. He had worked with Frege and Russell in the new methods of formal logic, which became the basis of a movement that attempted to repudiate idealism and the supposed excesses of German metaphysics. It used to be common to apologize for Wittgenstein's interest in Schopenhauer as a youthful aberration. But it was certainly more than that. In the *Tractatus* Wittgenstein uses Schopenhauer's images when talking about the 'I': it is an extensionless point, like an eye that cannot see itself, a limit – not a part – of the world. The 'I' is not among the facts that make up the world. Nor is there any value in the world. Value, whether ethical or aesthetic, seems to come from an attitude to the world as whole, not to any particular facts within it. 'To view the world sub specie aeterni (under the aspect of eternity)' – another of Schopenhauer's ideas – 'is to view it as a whole', and this is a mystical feeling, says Wittgenstein. The well-known image of philosophy as the ladder which one discards after climbing it is also reminiscent of Schopenhauer's view of the relationship between philosophy and mysticism.

There hangs over the *Tractatus* the sense that it is about something that appears only obliquely in the text. Its author said that the meaning of the book was an 'ethical' one, and in the book it transpires that ethics cannot be put into propositions, but must show itself. Wittgenstein was clearly troubled by the thought that once the world had been described in language, the really big questions, such as what the 'I' was, how it related to the world, what the point of the world was, and where good and evil came from, were left entirely untouched. As he struggled with these issues, the map on which he attempted to plot them was provided to a large extent by Schopenhauer's philosophy. This is particularly clear from his early notebooks, where the repeated vocabulary of 'subject' and 'object', 'will' and 'representation', 'world' and 'I' acquires any semblance of intelligibility only when viewed as an attempt to think things through with Schopenhauer's help.

Another area where Wittgenstein was clearly influenced by Schopenhauer is the theory of action. From his earliest writings through to his mature works, Wittgenstein worried about whether there is a mental act of will that is separate from bodily movement. The problem became central to his examination of whether the mental was in any sense 'hidden', and had a big influence on action-theory in analytical philosophy. The basic idea that Wittgenstein often seems drawn to is that willing is identical with acting, rather than being some purely 'inner' mental process. It is easy to see that this idea is essentially Schopenhauer's, and, although he does not mention his predecessor's name very often in this connection, the terms in which he discusses it reflect its ancestry.

Apart from the arts and philosophy, Schopenhauer's influence also extends into psychology, through his conception of the unconscious and his idea that sexuality is at the basis of personality. A very popular work in its day, now more or less forgotten, was Eduard von Hartmann's *Philosophy of the Unconscious* of 1869. This was a strange hybrid in which the author tried to combine some of Schopenhauer's ideas with some of Hegel's, and attempted a kind of *rapprochement* between optimism and pessimism. His chief modification of Schopenhauer's notion of the unconscious was to suggest that it must comprise not only will but also Idea, and somehow be in pursuit of rational ends. This work made the unconscious a theme for widespread study in the latter part of the nineteenth century, and served at the same time as a kind of channel for interest in Schopenhauer. Although Schopenhauer was not the first or only philosopher to discuss the unconscious, he probably made the greatest contribution before Freud.

Freud himself certainly consulted Hartmann's work and does make reference to it. It has often been pointed out, too, that he must have been familiar with Schopenhauer's ideas from the academic environment in which he moved. Nevertheless, Freud tried to distance himself from Schopenhauer, saying, in a well-known passage,

> I have carefully avoided any contact with philosophy proper. The large extent to which psycho-analysis coincides with the philosophy of Schopenhauer – not only did he assert the dominance of the emotions and the supreme importance of sexuality but he was even aware of the

mechanism of repression – is not to be traced to my acquaintance with his teaching. I read Schopenhauer very late in my life.

One almost hesitates to point out that Freud must have known at some level what to avoid reading, in order to preserve this title to originality. In any case, it is pretty certain that the great attention paid to Schopenhauer in academic and cultural life during this period was an important factor in making Freud's work possible, whether he was aware of it or not.

C. G. Jung is another influential psychologist who was impressed by Schopenhauer. He reports that he read Schopenhauer from his seventeenth year on (putting us, again, in the 1890s), and agreed with his picture of the world as full of confusion, passion, and evil: 'Here at last was someone who had courage for the insight that somehow the foundation of the world was not in the best of ways.'

Though Schopenhauer's metaphysics is not credible as a system, his questions about the self and the unconscious, action, striving, suffering, renunciation, aesthetic elevation, and the value of existence – the troubling or consoling thoughts that have excited so many influential thinkers – remain alive and challenging. As we debate the same issues with, perhaps, Nietzsche or Freud more prominently in the foreground, Schopenhauer's is a unique and powerful philosophical voice that still deserves to be heard.

Further reading

In addition to the standard translations of Schopenhauer's works listed in the 'Abbreviations and works cited' section at the beginning of the book, the following recent translations of Schopenhauer's works are also worth consulting:

Prize Essay on the Freedom of the Will, tr. E. F. J. Payne, ed. Günter Zöller (Cambridge University Press, 1999). For most purposes this would now supersede the Kolenda translation.

On Vision and Colors, tr. E. F. J. Payne, ed. David Cartwright (Berg Publishers, 1994)

Schopenhauer's Early Fourfold Root, translation and commentary F. C. White (Avebury, 1997). The less common but more accessible first edition of *The Fourfold Root*.

The World as Will and Idea (abridged in one volume), tr. Jill Berman, ed. David Berman (Dent, 1995). A much shortened version, which is more accessible than the standard Payne translation, but loses the larger architecture of Schopenhauer's main work.

And, in a new edition:

On the Basis of Morality, tr. E. F. J. Payne, with an introduction by David E. Cartwright (Berghahn Books, 1995)

A classical philosophical account of Schopenhauer, recently reprinted:

Patrick Gardiner, *Schopenhauer* (Penguin Books, 1967; repr. Thoemmes
    Press, 1997)

Other general accounts of Schopenhauer's philosophy:

D. W. Hamlyn, *Schopenhauer* (Routledge and Kegan Paul, 1980)
Julian Young, *Willing and Unwilling: A Study in the Philosophy of Arthur
    Schopenhauer* (Martinus Nijhoff, 1987)

A collection of scholarly articles on different aspects of Schopenhauer's
philosophy:

Christopher Janaway (ed.), *The Cambridge Companion to Schopenhauer*
    (Cambridge University Press, 1999)

Books and collections with more specialized focus:

John E. Atwell, *Schopenhauer: The Human Character* (Temple University
    Press, 1990)
John E. Atwell, *Schopenhauer on the Character of the World: The
    Metaphysics of Will* (University of California Press, 1995)
Dale Jacquette (ed.), *Schopenhauer, Philosophy and the Arts* (Cambridge
    University Press, 1996)
Christopher Janaway, *Self and World in Schopenhauer's Philosophy*
    (Clarendon Press, 1989)
Christopher Janaway (ed.), *Willing and Nothingness: Schopenhauer as
    Nietzsche's Educator* (Clarendon Press, 1998)
F. C. White, *On Schopenhauer's Fourfold Root of the Principle of
    Sufficient Reason* (E. J. Brill, 1992)

Three different accounts of Schopenhauer's life, work, and place in
intellectual history:

Arthur Hübscher, *The Philosophy of Schopenhauer in its Intellectual*

Context: Thinker Against the Tide, tr. Joachim T. Baer and David E. Cartwright (Edwin Mellen Press, 1989)

Bryan Magee, *The Philosophy of Schopenhauer*, 2nd edn. (Clarendon Press, 1997)

Rüdiger Safranski, *Schopenhauer and the Wild Years of Philosophy* (Weidenfeld & Nicolson, 1989)

Index

Visit the
VERY SHORT INTRODUCTIONS
Web site

www.oup.co.uk/vsi

➤ **Information** about all published titles

➤ News of **forthcoming books**

➤ **Extracts** from the books, including titles not yet published

➤ **Reviews** and views

➤ **Links** to other **web sites** and main OUP web page

➤ Information about **VSIs in translation**

➤ **Contact** the editors

➤ **Order** other **VSIs** on-line

CONTINENTAL PHILOSOPHY
A Very Short Introduction
Simon Critchley

Continental philosophy is a contested concept which cuts to the heart of the identity of philosophy and its relevance to matters of public concern and personal life. This book attempts to answer the question 'What is Continental philosophy?' by telling a story that began with Kant 200 years ago and includes discussions of major philosophers like Nietzsche, Husserl and Heidegger. At the core of the book is a plea to place philosophy at the centre of cultural life, and thus reawaken its ancient definition of the love of wisdom that makes life worth living.

> 'Antagonism and mutual misrepresentation between so-called analytical and continental philosophy have helped shape the course of every significant development in Western intellectual life since the 1960s – structuralism, post-structuralism, postmodernism, gender studies, etc. Simon Critchley has skilfully and sympathetically sketched continental lines of thought so that strangers to their detail may enter them systematically enough that their principle texts begin to illuminate one another. It is a remarkable achievement.'

> **Stanley Cavell, Harvard University**

www.oup.co.uk/isbn/0-19-285359-7